**I DRAW FASHION**

# OVAL
# FACE SHAPE

## MAKEUP FACE CHARTS
## FOR MAKEUP ARTISTS

MODEL: WHITE

# CONTENTS

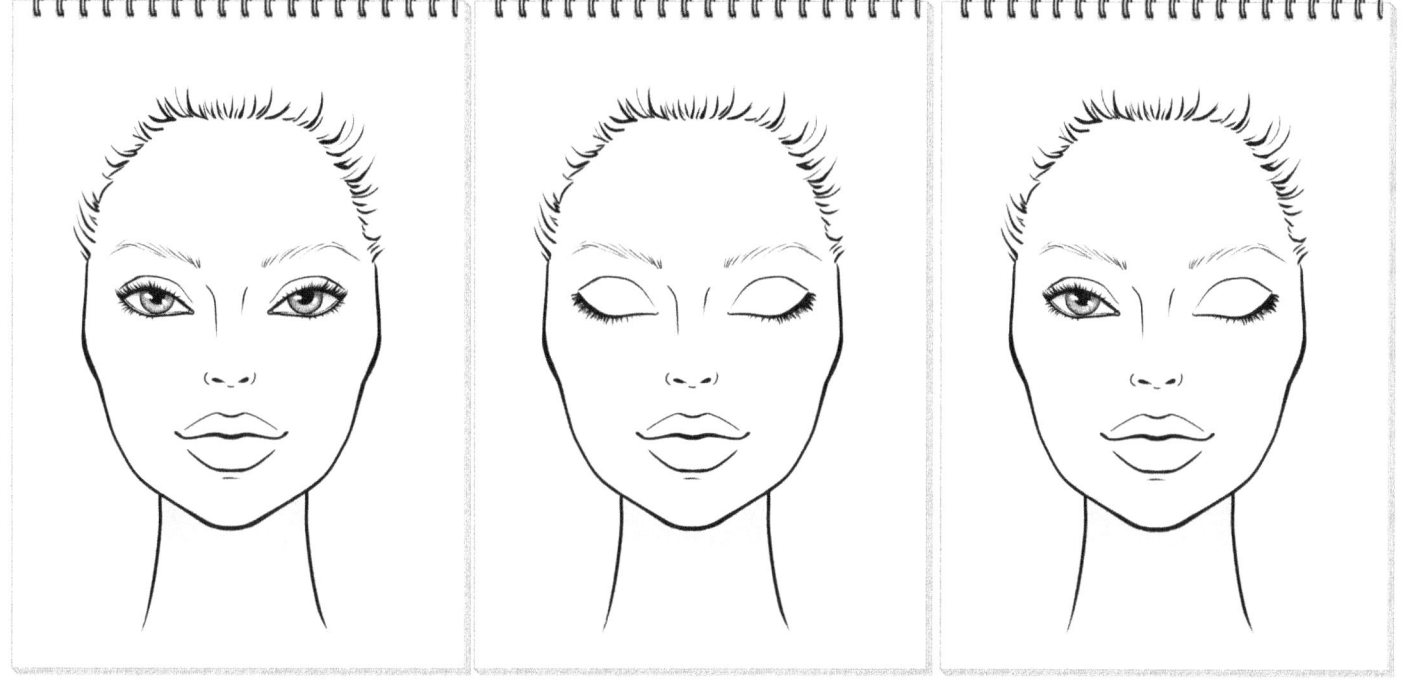

# OPENED EYES
# FACE CHARTS

## PREPARATION

Cleanser

------------------------------------

Moisturizer

------------------------------------

Primer

------------------------------------

## FACE

Concealer

------------------------------------

Foundation

------------------------------------

Powder

------------------------------------

Highlighter

------------------------------------

Contour

------------------------------------

Bronzer

------------------------------------

Blush

------------------------------------

## EYES

Eyeshadow lid

------------------------------------

Eyeshadow crease

------------------------------------

Eyeliner

------------------------------------

Mascara

------------------------------------

Lashes

------------------------------------

Brows

------------------------------------

## LIPS

Lip color

------------------------------------

Lip liner

------------------------------------

Lip gloss

------------------------------------

## OTHER

------------------------------------

------------------------------------

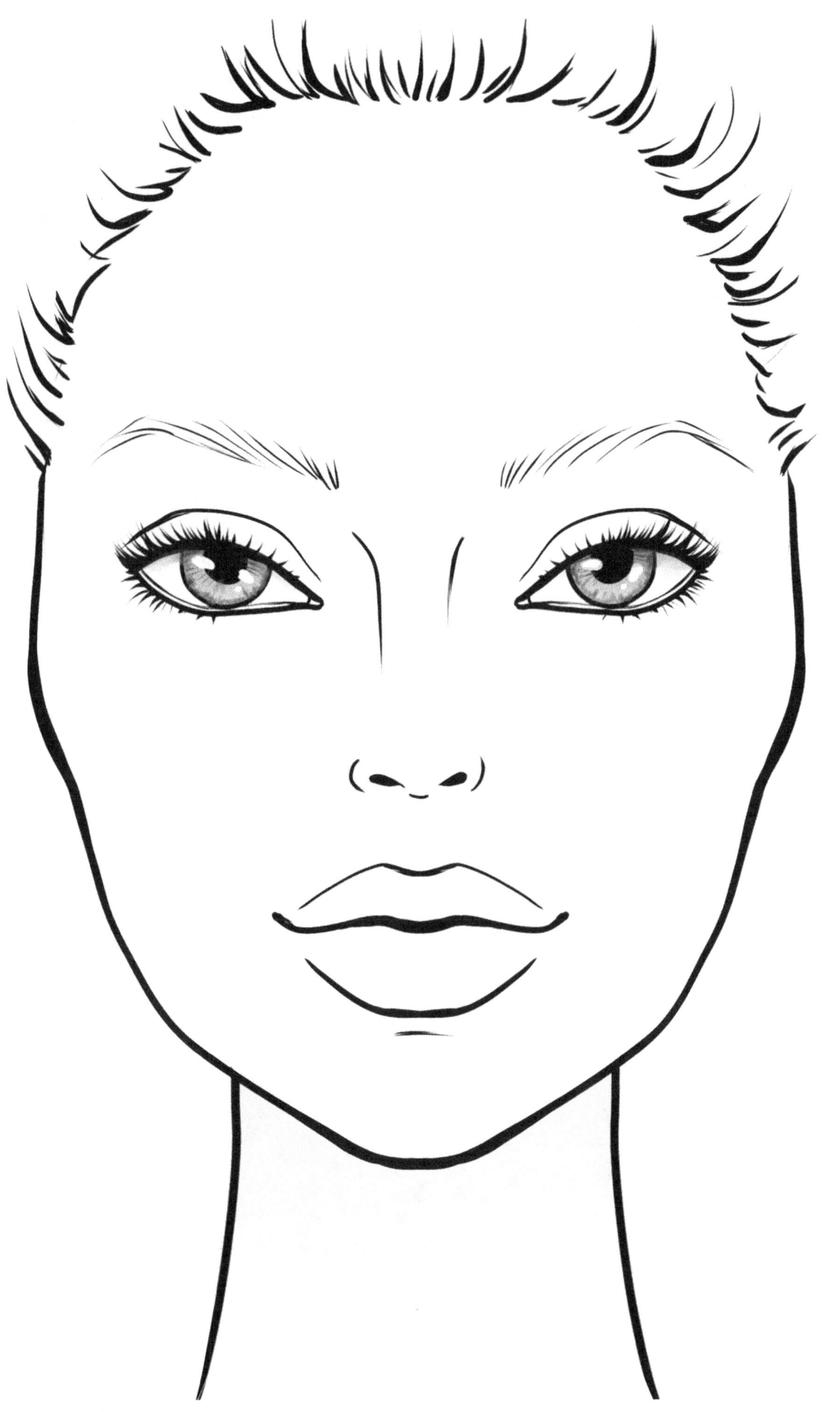

## PREPARATION

Cleanser

------------------------------------

Moisturizer

------------------------------------

Primer

------------------------------------

## FACE

Concealer

------------------------------------

Foundation

------------------------------------

Powder

------------------------------------

Highlighter

------------------------------------

Contour

------------------------------------

Bronzer

------------------------------------

Blush

------------------------------------

## EYES

Eyeshadow lid

------------------------------------

Eyeshadow crease

------------------------------------

Eyeliner

------------------------------------

Mascara

------------------------------------

Lashes

------------------------------------

Brows

------------------------------------

## LIPS

Lip color

------------------------------------

Lip liner

------------------------------------

Lip gloss

------------------------------------

## OTHER

------------------------------------

------------------------------------

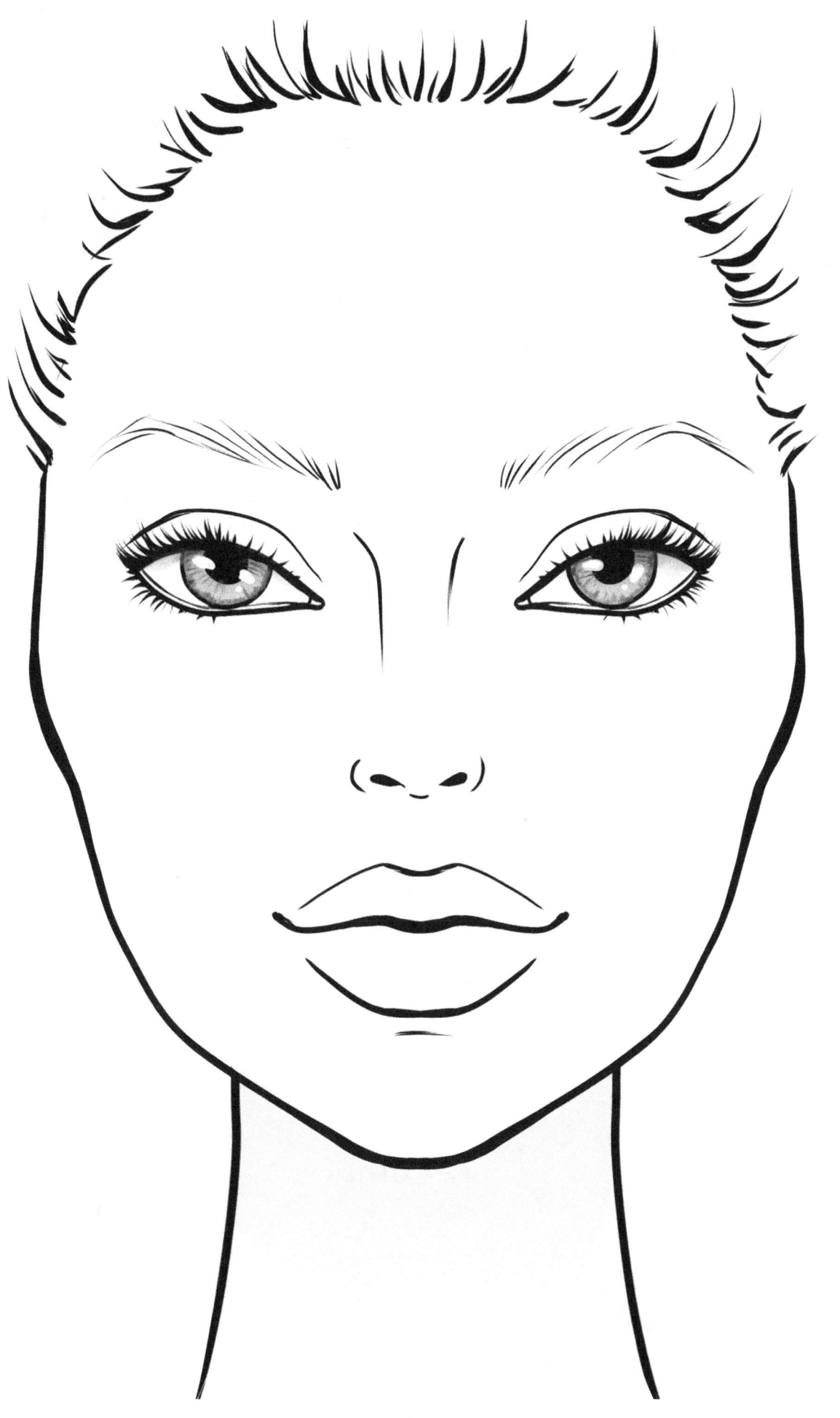

## PREPARATION

Cleanser

---

Moisturizer

---

Primer

---

## FACE

Concealer

---

Foundation

---

Powder

---

Highlighter

---

Contour

---

Bronzer

---

Blush

---

## EYES

Eyeshadow lid

---

Eyeshadow crease

---

Eyeliner

---

Mascara

---

Lashes

---

Brows

---

## LIPS

Lip color

---

Lip liner

---

Lip gloss

---

## OTHER

---

---

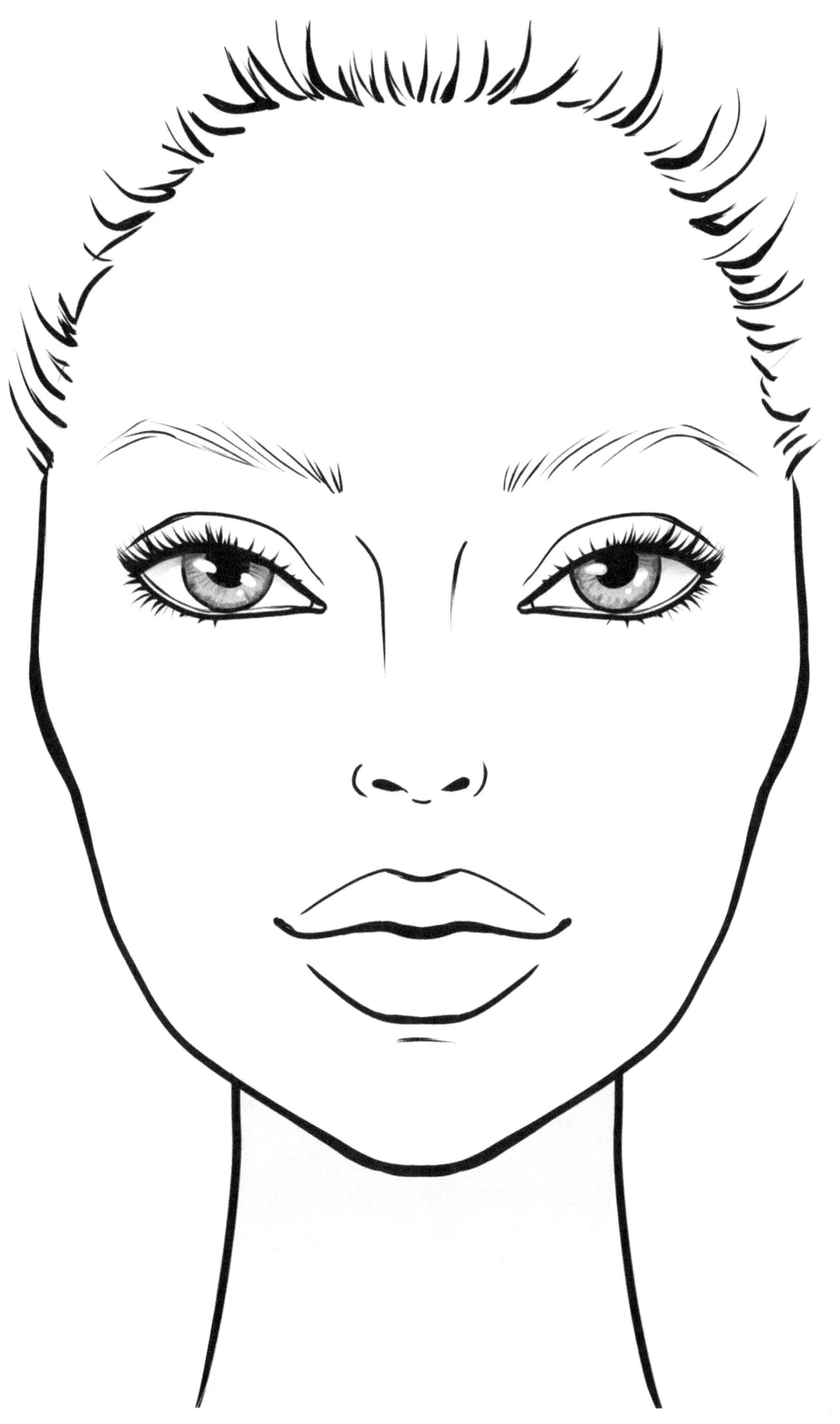

## PREPARATION

Cleanser

---

Moisturizer

---

Primer

---

## FACE

Concealer

---

Foundation

---

Powder

---

Highlighter

---

Contour

---

Bronzer

---

Blush

---

## EYES

Eyeshadow lid

---

Eyeshadow crease

---

Eyeliner

---

Mascara

---

Lashes

---

Brows

---

## LIPS

Lip color

---

Lip liner

---

Lip gloss

---

## OTHER

---

---

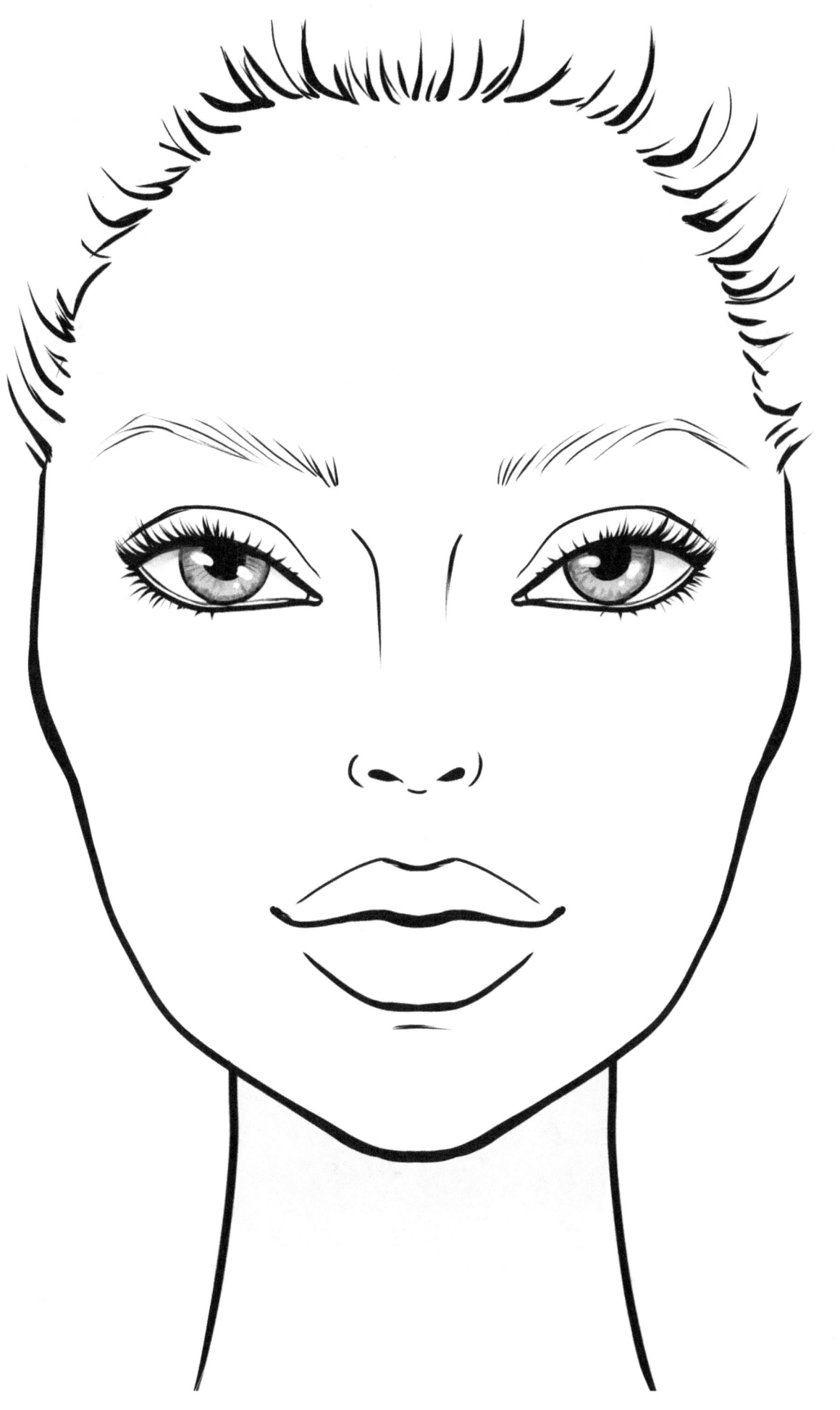

## PREPARATION

Cleanser

------------------------------------

Moisturizer

------------------------------------

Primer

------------------------------------

## FACE

Concealer

------------------------------------

Foundation

------------------------------------

Powder

------------------------------------

Highlighter

------------------------------------

Contour

------------------------------------

Bronzer

------------------------------------

Blush

------------------------------------

## EYES

Eyeshadow lid

------------------------------------

Eyeshadow crease

------------------------------------

Eyeliner

------------------------------------

Mascara

------------------------------------

Lashes

------------------------------------

Brows

------------------------------------

## LIPS

Lip color

------------------------------------

Lip liner

------------------------------------

Lip gloss

------------------------------------

## OTHER

------------------------------------

------------------------------------

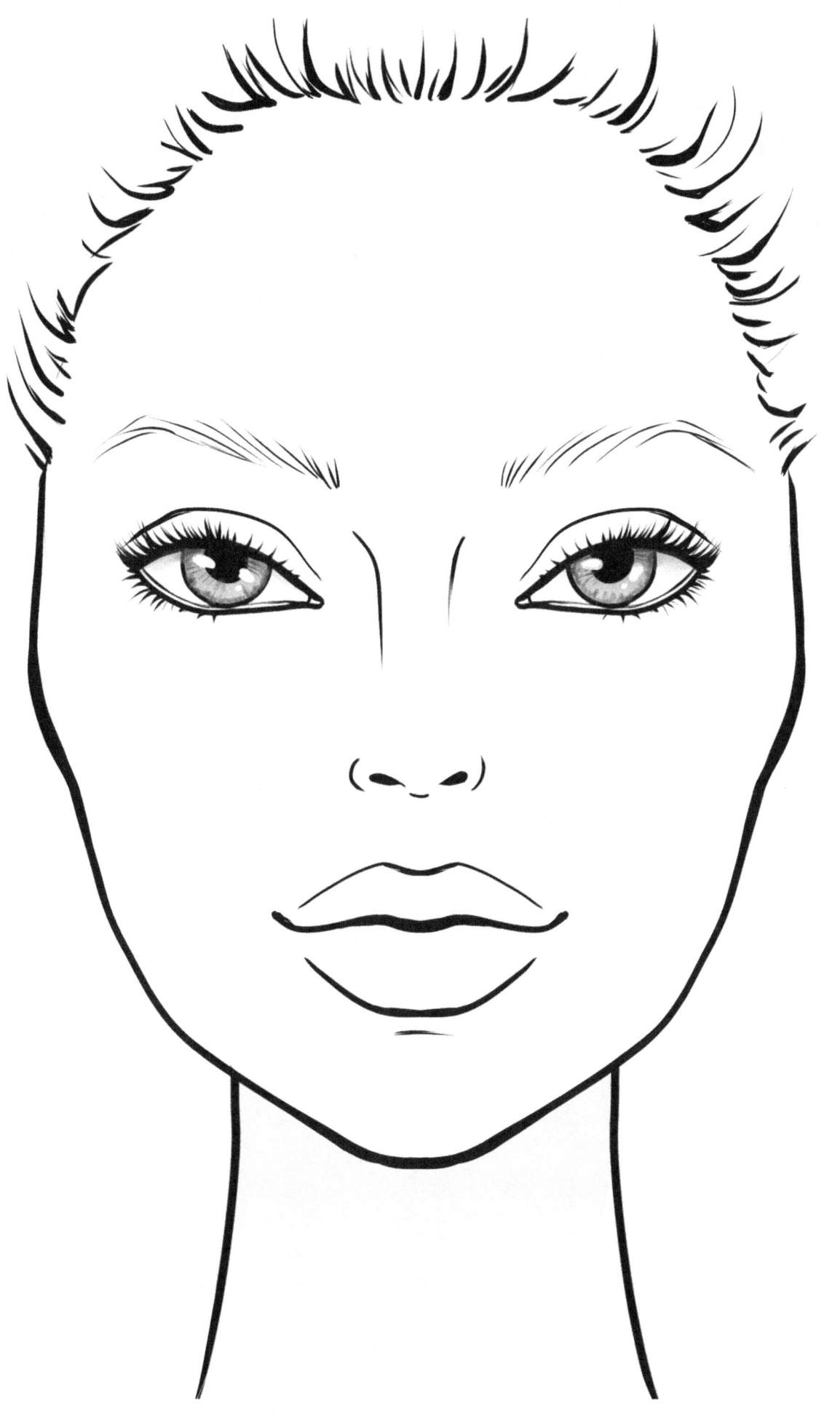

## PREPARATION

Cleanser

------------------------------

Moisturizer

------------------------------

Primer

------------------------------

## FACE

Concealer

------------------------------

Foundation

------------------------------

Powder

------------------------------

Highlighter

------------------------------

Contour

------------------------------

Bronzer

------------------------------

Blush

------------------------------

## EYES

Eyeshadow lid

------------------------------

Eyeshadow crease

------------------------------

Eyeliner

------------------------------

Mascara

------------------------------

Lashes

------------------------------

Brows

------------------------------

## LIPS

Lip color

------------------------------

Lip liner

------------------------------

Lip gloss

------------------------------

## OTHER

------------------------------

------------------------------

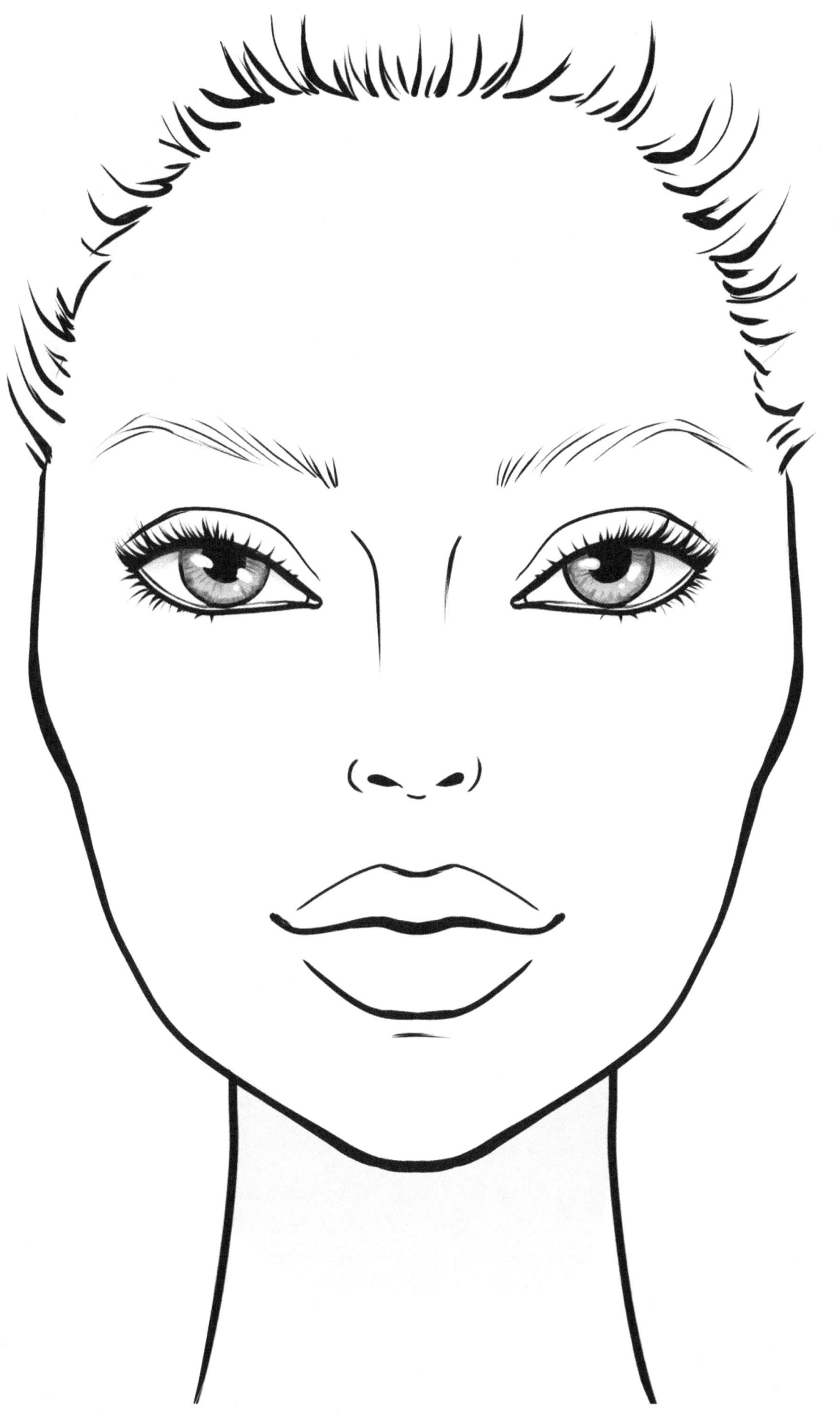

## PREPARATION

Cleanser

---

Moisturizer

---

Primer

---

## FACE

Concealer

---

Foundation

---

Powder

---

Highlighter

---

Contour

---

Bronzer

---

Blush

---

## EYES

Eyeshadow lid

---

Eyeshadow crease

---

Eyeliner

---

Mascara

---

Lashes

---

Brows

---

## LIPS

Lip color

---

Lip liner

---

Lip gloss

---

## OTHER

---

---

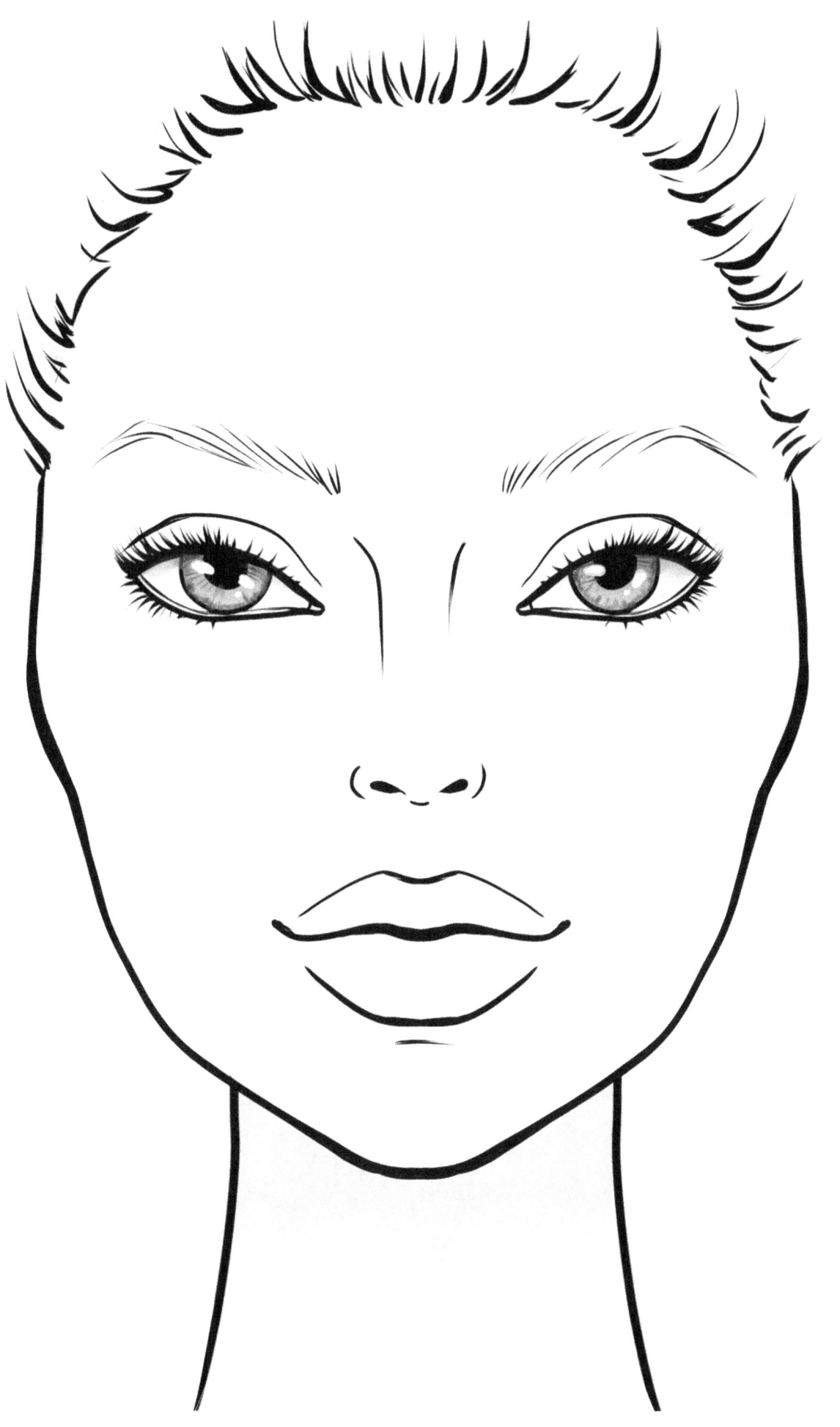

## PREPARATION

Cleanser

----------------------------------------

Moisturizer

----------------------------------------

Primer

----------------------------------------

## FACE

Concealer

----------------------------------------

Foundation

----------------------------------------

Powder

----------------------------------------

Highlighter

----------------------------------------

Contour

----------------------------------------

Bronzer

----------------------------------------

Blush

----------------------------------------

## EYES

Eyeshadow lid

----------------------------------------

Eyeshadow crease

----------------------------------------

Eyeliner

----------------------------------------

Mascara

----------------------------------------

Lashes

----------------------------------------

Brows

----------------------------------------

## LIPS

Lip color

----------------------------------------

Lip liner

----------------------------------------

Lip gloss

----------------------------------------

## OTHER

----------------------------------------

----------------------------------------

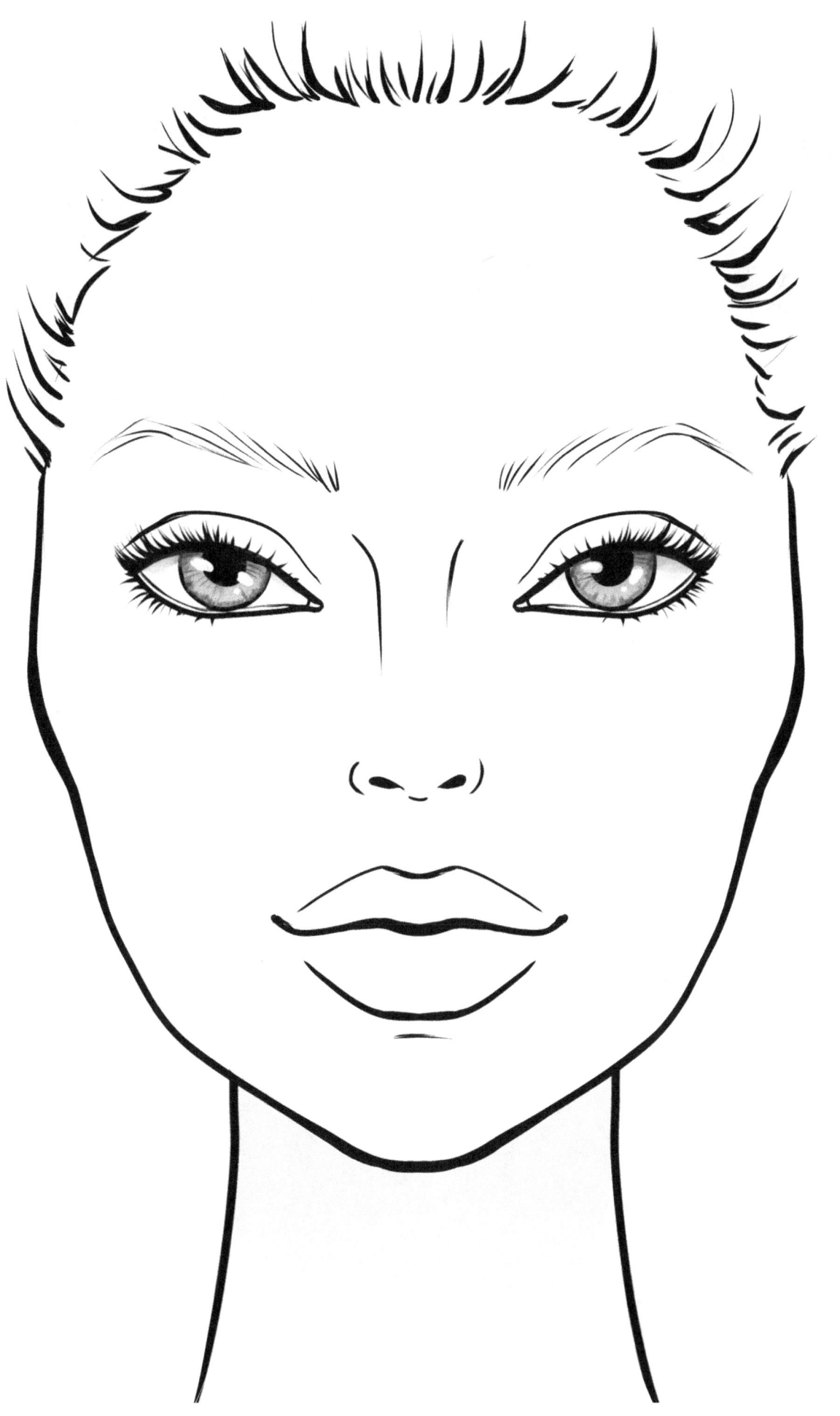

## PREPARATION

Cleanser

----------------------------------------

Moisturizer

----------------------------------------

Primer

----------------------------------------

## FACE

Concealer

----------------------------------------

Foundation

----------------------------------------

Powder

----------------------------------------

Highlighter

----------------------------------------

Contour

----------------------------------------

Bronzer

----------------------------------------

Blush

----------------------------------------

## EYES

Eyeshadow lid

----------------------------------------

Eyeshadow crease

----------------------------------------

Eyeliner

----------------------------------------

Mascara

----------------------------------------

Lashes

----------------------------------------

Brows

----------------------------------------

## LIPS

Lip color

----------------------------------------

Lip liner

----------------------------------------

Lip gloss

----------------------------------------

## OTHER

----------------------------------------

----------------------------------------

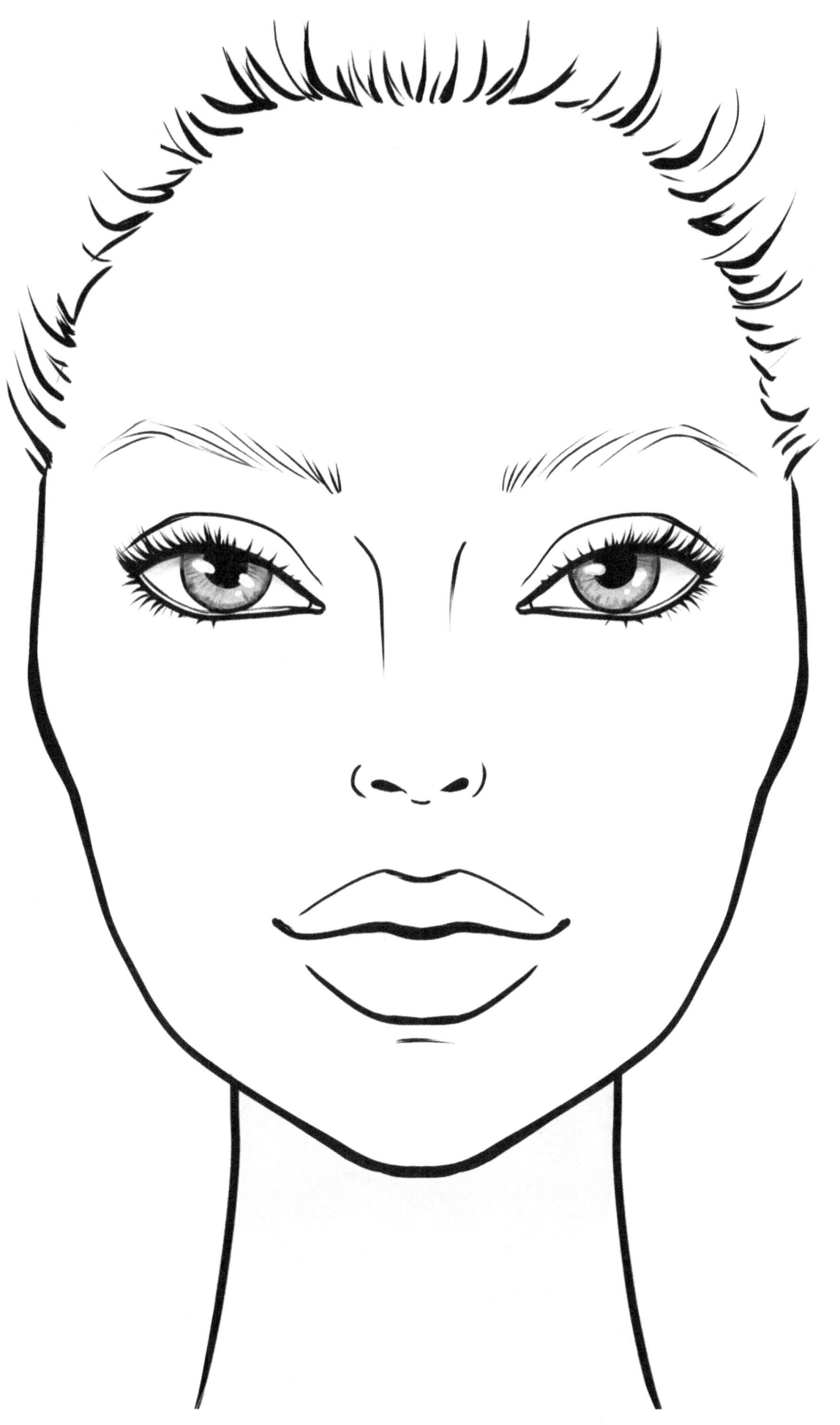

## PREPARATION

Cleanser

------------------------------------

Moisturizer

------------------------------------

Primer

------------------------------------

## FACE

Concealer

------------------------------------

Foundation

------------------------------------

Powder

------------------------------------

Highlighter

------------------------------------

Contour

------------------------------------

Bronzer

------------------------------------

Blush

------------------------------------

## EYES

Eyeshadow lid

------------------------------------

Eyeshadow crease

------------------------------------

Eyeliner

------------------------------------

Mascara

------------------------------------

Lashes

------------------------------------

Brows

------------------------------------

## LIPS

Lip color

------------------------------------

Lip liner

------------------------------------

Lip gloss

------------------------------------

## OTHER

------------------------------------

------------------------------------

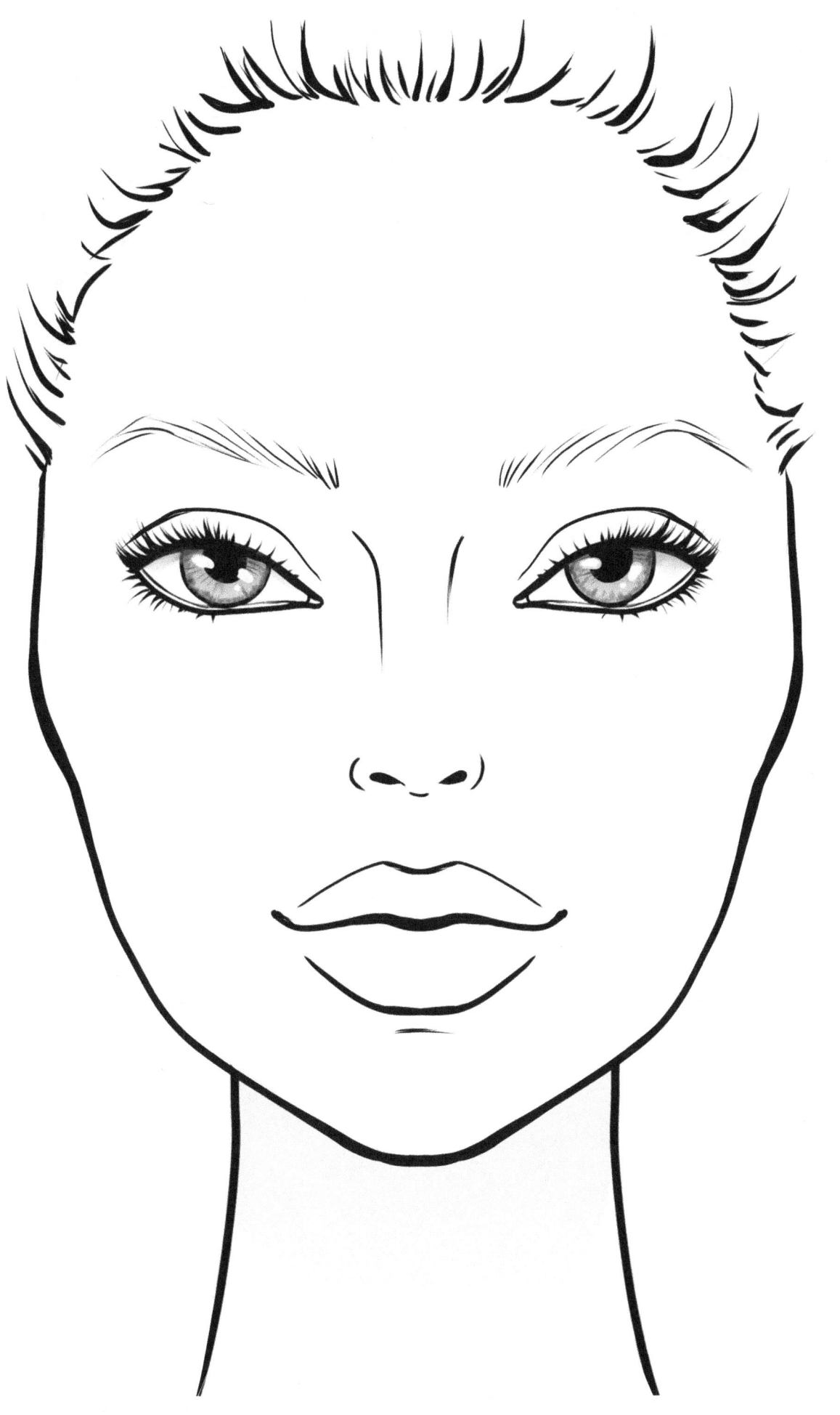

## PREPARATION

Cleanser
---------------------------------

Moisturizer
---------------------------------

Primer
---------------------------------

## FACE

Concealer
---------------------------------

Foundation
---------------------------------

Powder
---------------------------------

Highlighter
---------------------------------

Contour
---------------------------------

Bronzer
---------------------------------

Blush
---------------------------------

## EYES

Eyeshadow lid
---------------------------------

Eyeshadow crease
---------------------------------

Eyeliner
---------------------------------

Mascara
---------------------------------

Lashes
---------------------------------

Brows
---------------------------------

## LIPS

Lip color
---------------------------------

Lip liner
---------------------------------

Lip gloss
---------------------------------

## OTHER

---------------------------------

---------------------------------

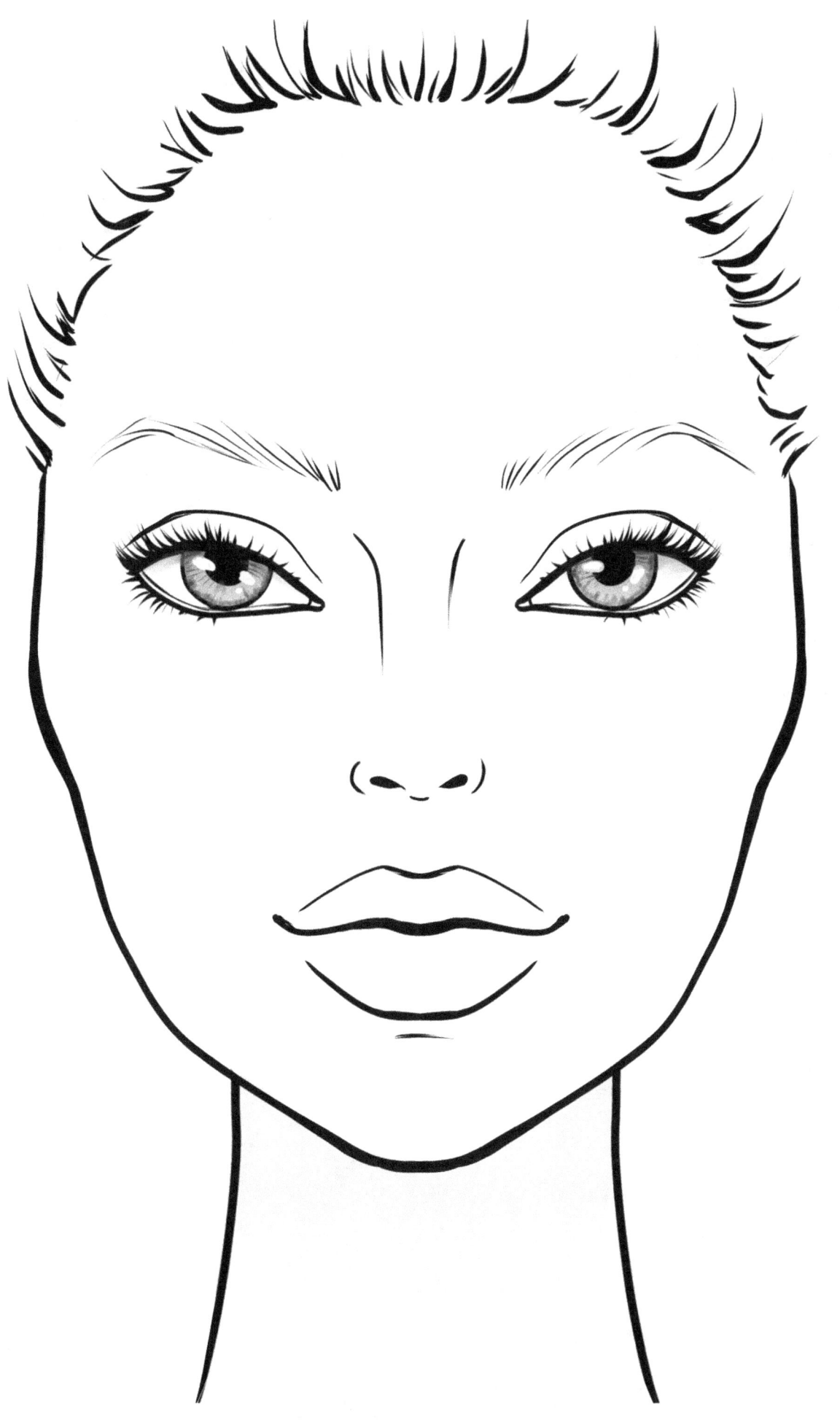

## PREPARATION

Cleanser

-------------------------------------------------

Moisturizer

-------------------------------------------------

Primer

-------------------------------------------------

## FACE

Concealer

-------------------------------------------------

Foundation

-------------------------------------------------

Powder

-------------------------------------------------

Highlighter

-------------------------------------------------

Contour

-------------------------------------------------

Bronzer

-------------------------------------------------

Blush

-------------------------------------------------

## EYES

Eyeshadow lid

-------------------------------------------------

Eyeshadow crease

-------------------------------------------------

Eyeliner

-------------------------------------------------

Mascara

-------------------------------------------------

Lashes

-------------------------------------------------

Brows

-------------------------------------------------

## LIPS

Lip color

-------------------------------------------------

Lip liner

-------------------------------------------------

Lip gloss

-------------------------------------------------

## OTHER

-------------------------------------------------

-------------------------------------------------

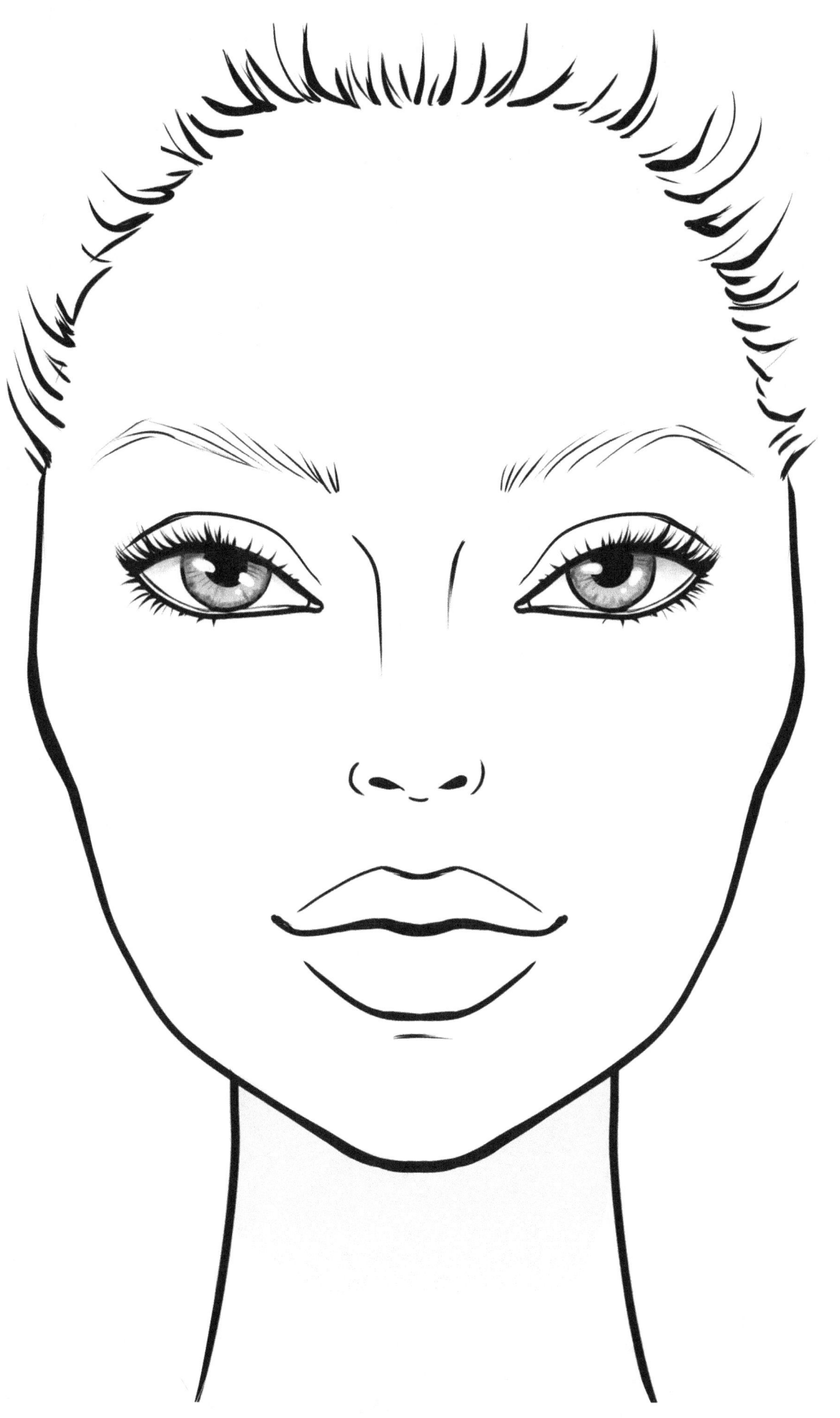

## PREPARATION

Cleanser

----------------------------------------

Moisturizer

----------------------------------------

Primer

----------------------------------------

## FACE

Concealer

----------------------------------------

Foundation

----------------------------------------

Powder

----------------------------------------

Highlighter

----------------------------------------

Contour

----------------------------------------

Bronzer

----------------------------------------

Blush

----------------------------------------

## EYES

Eyeshadow lid

----------------------------------------

Eyeshadow crease

----------------------------------------

Eyeliner

----------------------------------------

Mascara

----------------------------------------

Lashes

----------------------------------------

Brows

----------------------------------------

## LIPS

Lip color

----------------------------------------

Lip liner

----------------------------------------

Lip gloss

----------------------------------------

## OTHER

----------------------------------------

----------------------------------------

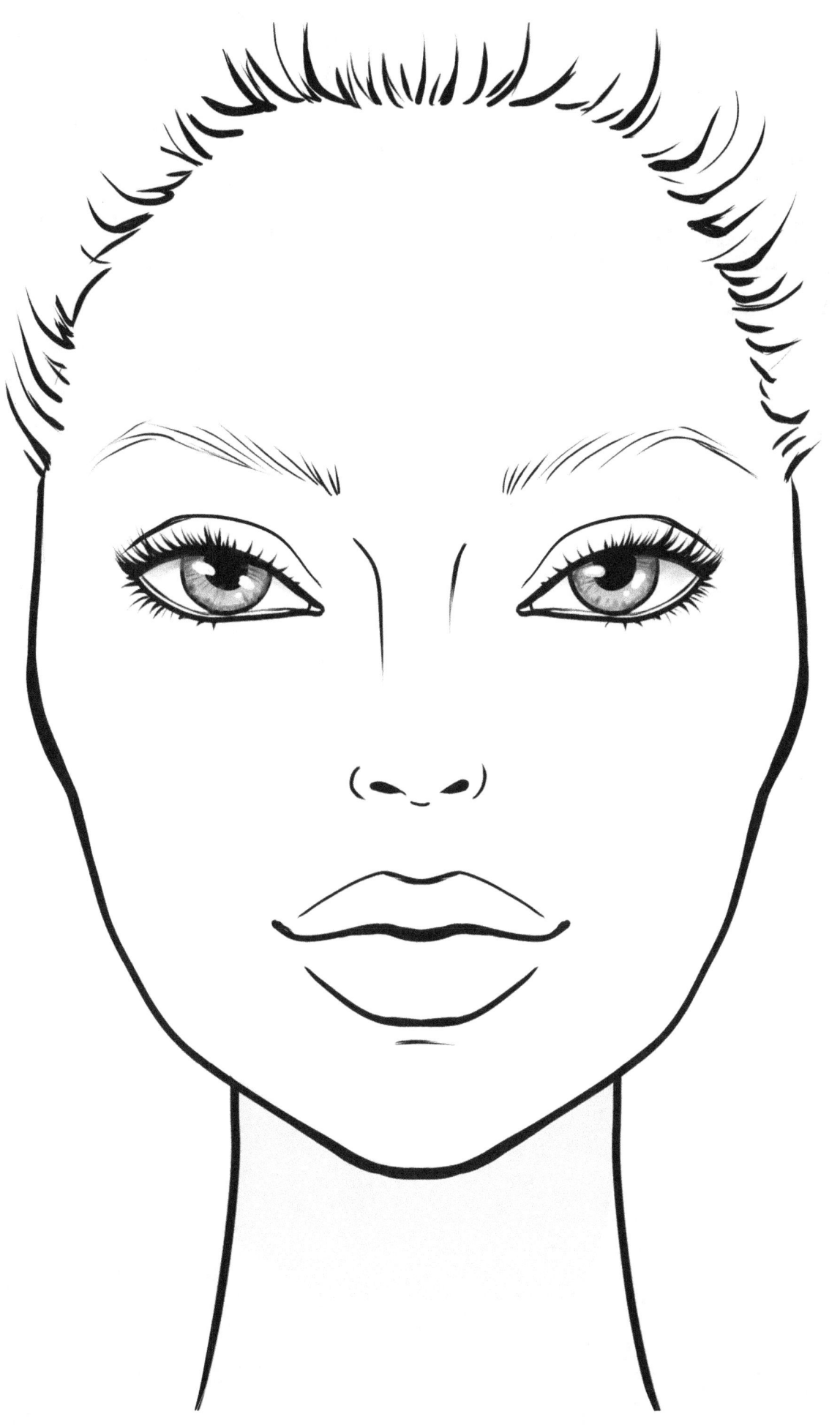

## PREPARATION

Cleanser

------------------------------------

Moisturizer

------------------------------------

Primer

------------------------------------

## FACE

Concealer

------------------------------------

Foundation

------------------------------------

Powder

------------------------------------

Highlighter

------------------------------------

Contour

------------------------------------

Bronzer

------------------------------------

Blush

------------------------------------

## EYES

Eyeshadow lid

------------------------------------

Eyeshadow crease

------------------------------------

Eyeliner

------------------------------------

Mascara

------------------------------------

Lashes

------------------------------------

Brows

------------------------------------

## LIPS

Lip color

------------------------------------

Lip liner

------------------------------------

Lip gloss

------------------------------------

## OTHER

------------------------------------

------------------------------------

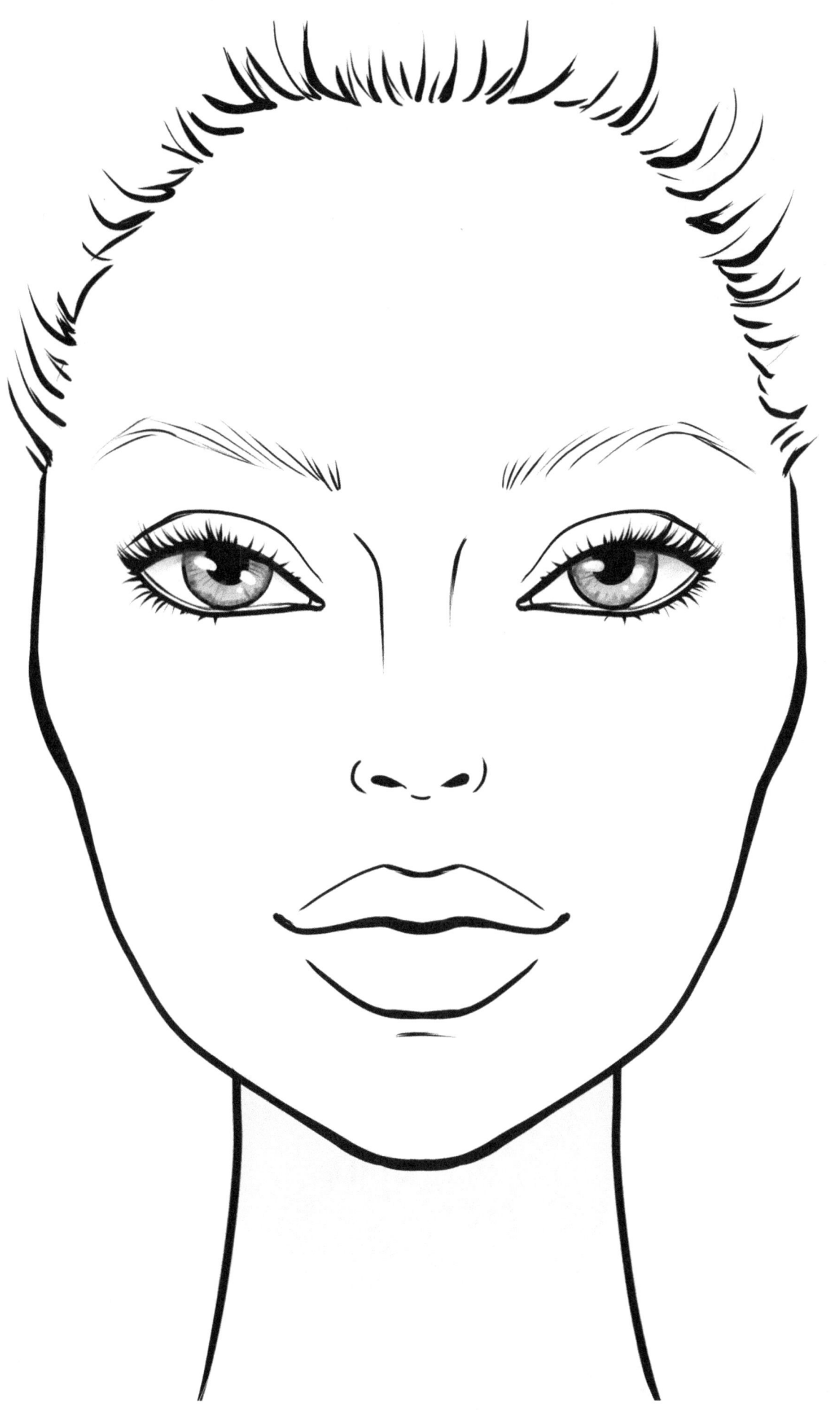

## PREPARATION

Cleanser

-------------------------------------

Moisturizer

-------------------------------------

Primer

-------------------------------------

## FACE

Concealer

-------------------------------------

Foundation

-------------------------------------

Powder

-------------------------------------

Highlighter

-------------------------------------

Contour

-------------------------------------

Bronzer

-------------------------------------

Blush

-------------------------------------

## EYES

Eyeshadow lid

-------------------------------------

Eyeshadow crease

-------------------------------------

Eyeliner

-------------------------------------

Mascara

-------------------------------------

Lashes

-------------------------------------

Brows

-------------------------------------

## LIPS

Lip color

-------------------------------------

Lip liner

-------------------------------------

Lip gloss

-------------------------------------

## OTHER

-------------------------------------

-------------------------------------

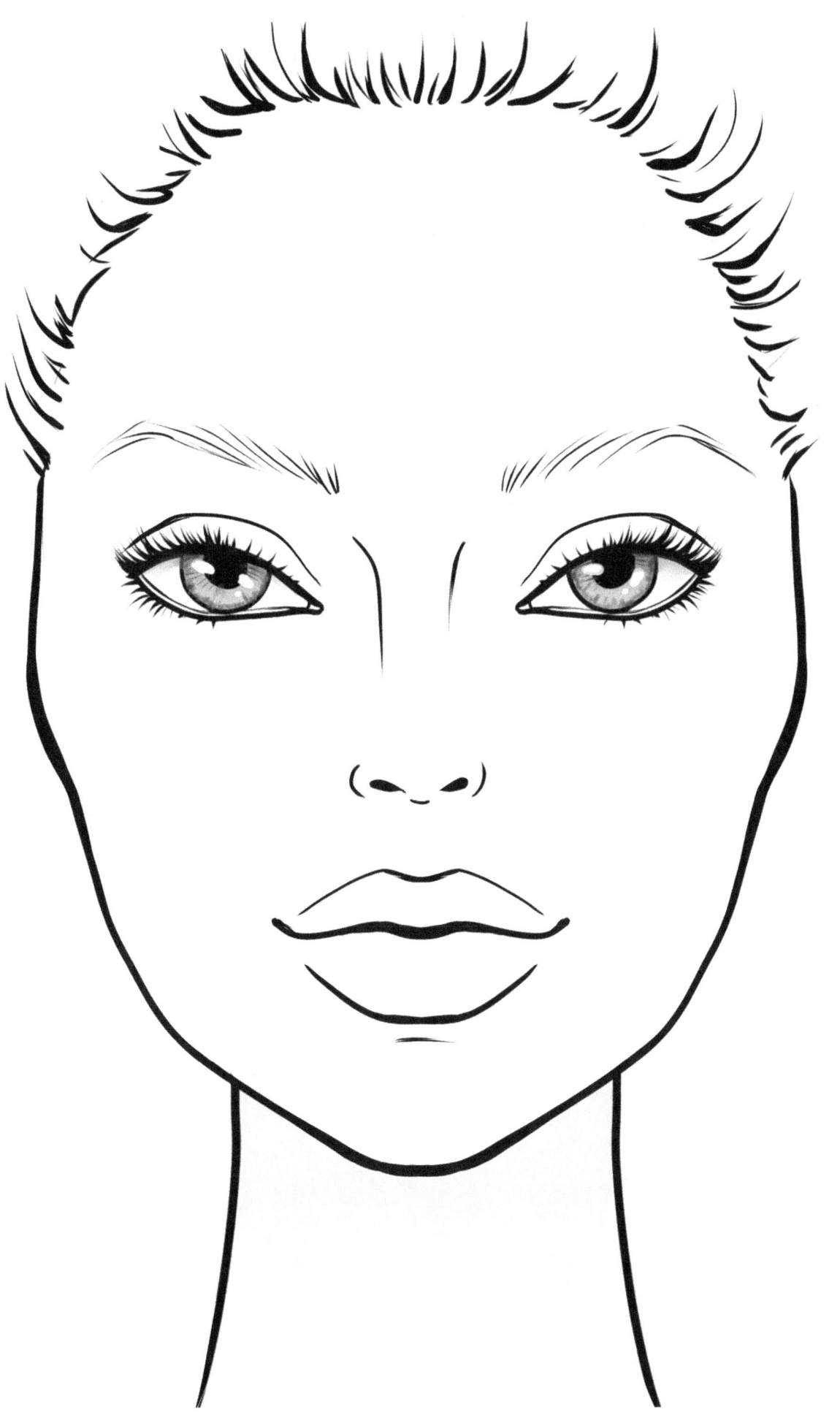

## PREPARATION

Cleanser

-------------------------------

Moisturizer

-------------------------------

Primer

-------------------------------

## FACE

Concealer

-------------------------------

Foundation

-------------------------------

Powder

-------------------------------

Highlighter

-------------------------------

Contour

-------------------------------

Bronzer

-------------------------------

Blush

-------------------------------

## EYES

Eyeshadow lid

-------------------------------

Eyeshadow crease

-------------------------------

Eyeliner

-------------------------------

Mascara

-------------------------------

Lashes

-------------------------------

Brows

-------------------------------

## LIPS

Lip color

-------------------------------

Lip liner

-------------------------------

Lip gloss

-------------------------------

## OTHER

-------------------------------

-------------------------------

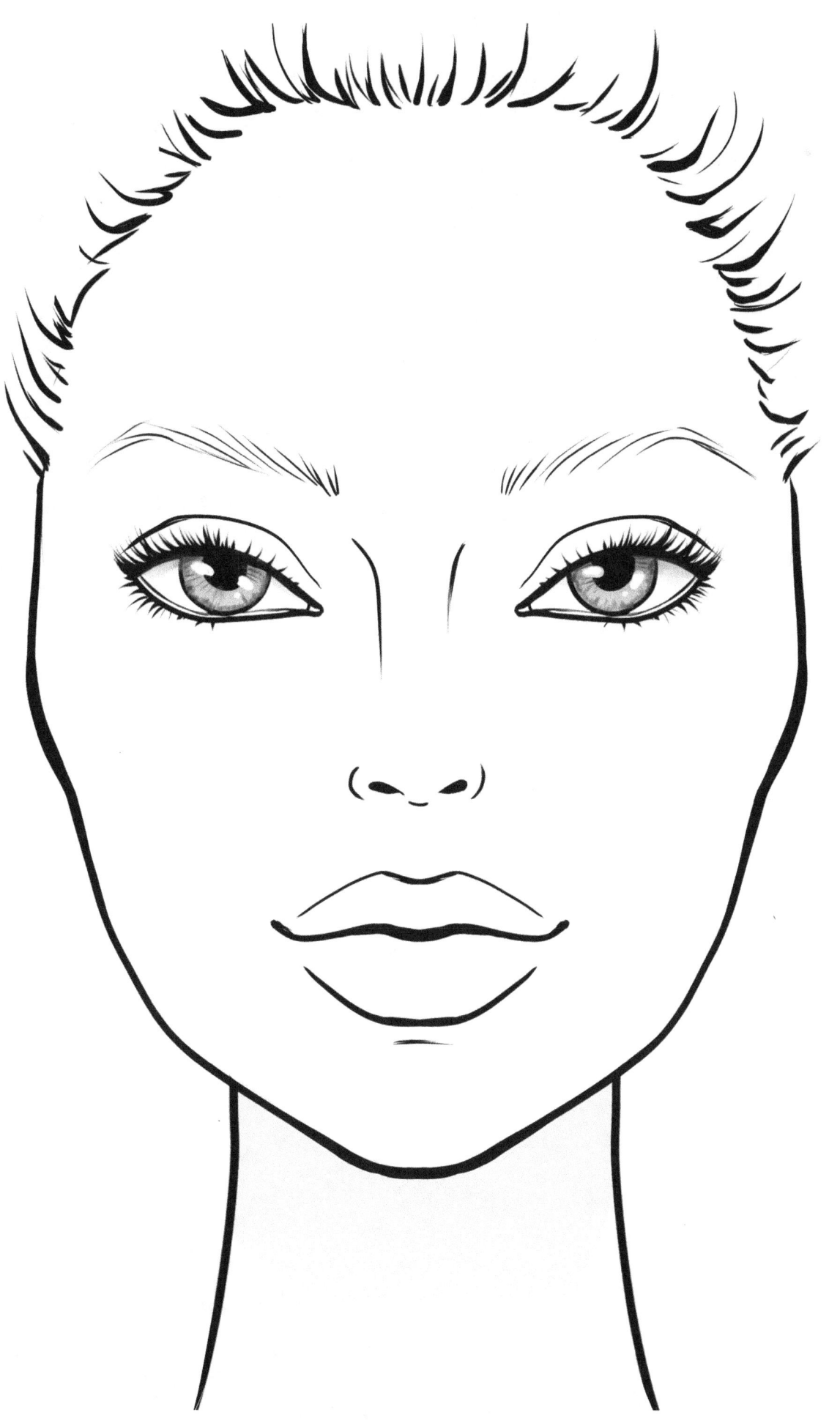

## PREPARATION

Cleanser

_____

Moisturizer

_____

Primer

_____

## FACE

Concealer

_____

Foundation

_____

Powder

_____

Highlighter

_____

Contour

_____

Bronzer

_____

Blush

_____

## EYES

Eyeshadow lid

_____

Eyeshadow crease

_____

Eyeliner

_____

Mascara

_____

Lashes

_____

Brows

_____

## LIPS

Lip color

_____

Lip liner

_____

Lip gloss

_____

## OTHER

_____

_____

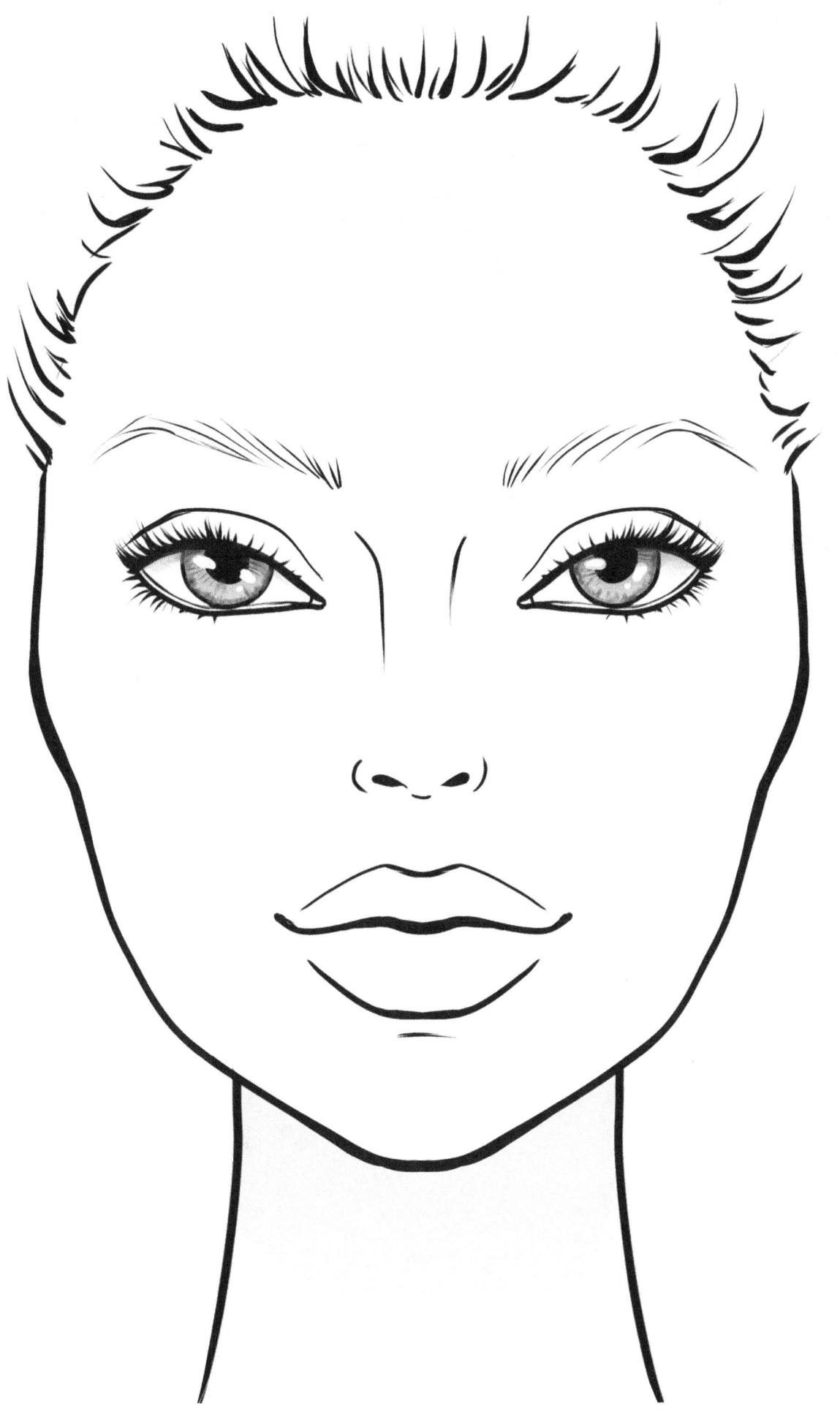

## PREPARATION

Cleanser

----------------------------------------

Moisturizer

----------------------------------------

Primer

----------------------------------------

## FACE

Concealer

----------------------------------------

Foundation

----------------------------------------

Powder

----------------------------------------

Highlighter

----------------------------------------

Contour

----------------------------------------

Bronzer

----------------------------------------

Blush

----------------------------------------

## EYES

Eyeshadow lid

----------------------------------------

Eyeshadow crease

----------------------------------------

Eyeliner

----------------------------------------

Mascara

----------------------------------------

Lashes

----------------------------------------

Brows

----------------------------------------

## LIPS

Lip color

----------------------------------------

Lip liner

----------------------------------------

Lip gloss

----------------------------------------

## OTHER

----------------------------------------

----------------------------------------

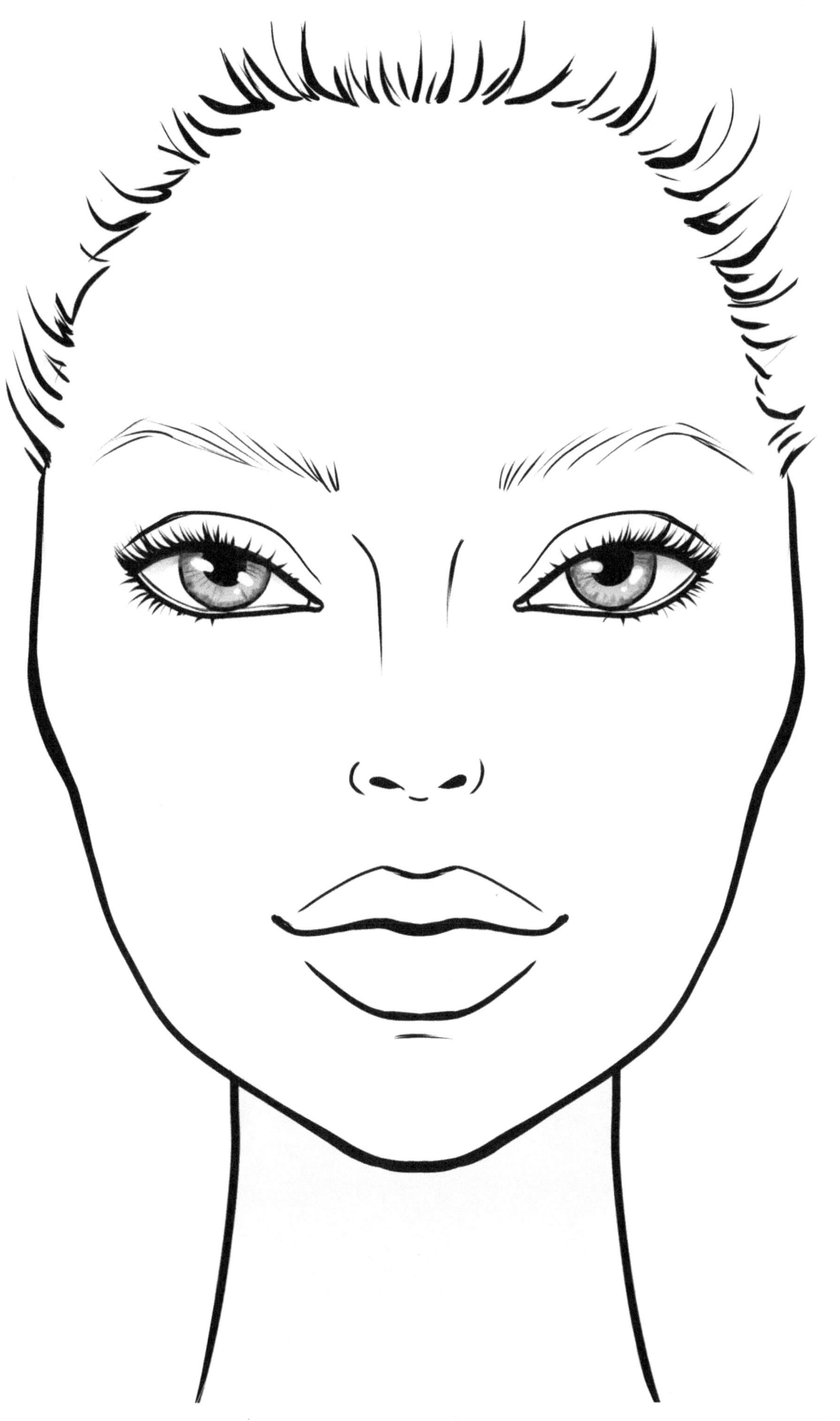

# ONE EYE OPENED, ONE EYE CLOSED FACE CHARTS

## PREPARATION

Cleanser

------------------------------------------------

Moisturizer

------------------------------------------------

Primer

------------------------------------------------

## FACE

Concealer

------------------------------------------------

Foundation

------------------------------------------------

Powder

------------------------------------------------

Highlighter

------------------------------------------------

Contour

------------------------------------------------

Bronzer

------------------------------------------------

Blush

------------------------------------------------

## EYES

Eyeshadow lid

------------------------------------------------

Eyeshadow crease

------------------------------------------------

Eyeliner

------------------------------------------------

Mascara

------------------------------------------------

Lashes

------------------------------------------------

Brows

------------------------------------------------

## LIPS

Lip color

------------------------------------------------

Lip liner

------------------------------------------------

Lip gloss

------------------------------------------------

## OTHER

------------------------------------------------

------------------------------------------------

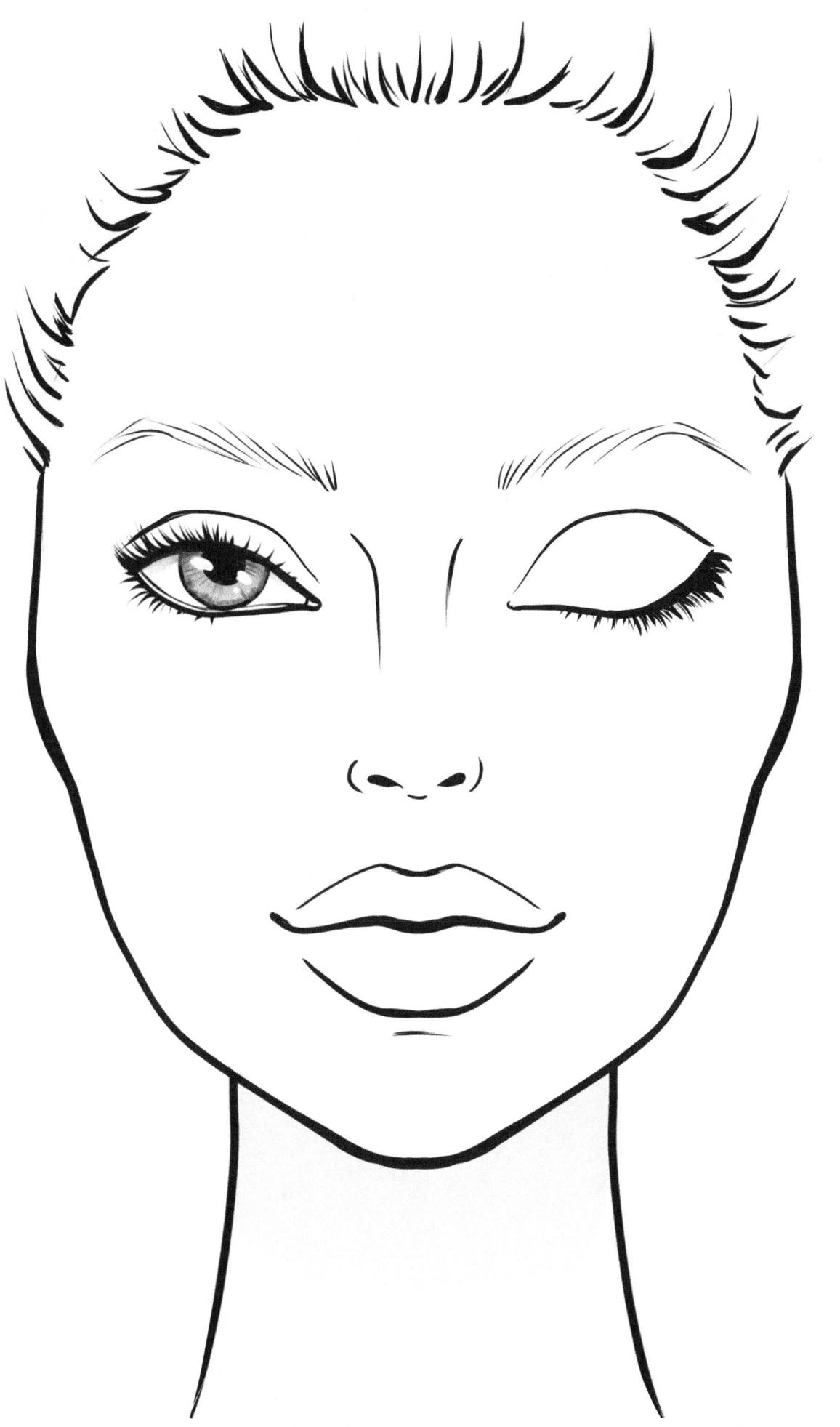

## PREPARATION

Cleanser

-------------------------------------

Moisturizer

-------------------------------------

Primer

-------------------------------------

## FACE

Concealer

-------------------------------------

Foundation

-------------------------------------

Powder

-------------------------------------

Highlighter

-------------------------------------

Contour

-------------------------------------

Bronzer

-------------------------------------

Blush

-------------------------------------

## EYES

Eyeshadow lid

-------------------------------------

Eyeshadow crease

-------------------------------------

Eyeliner

-------------------------------------

Mascara

-------------------------------------

Lashes

-------------------------------------

Brows

-------------------------------------

## LIPS

Lip color

-------------------------------------

Lip liner

-------------------------------------

Lip gloss

-------------------------------------

## OTHER

-------------------------------------

-------------------------------------

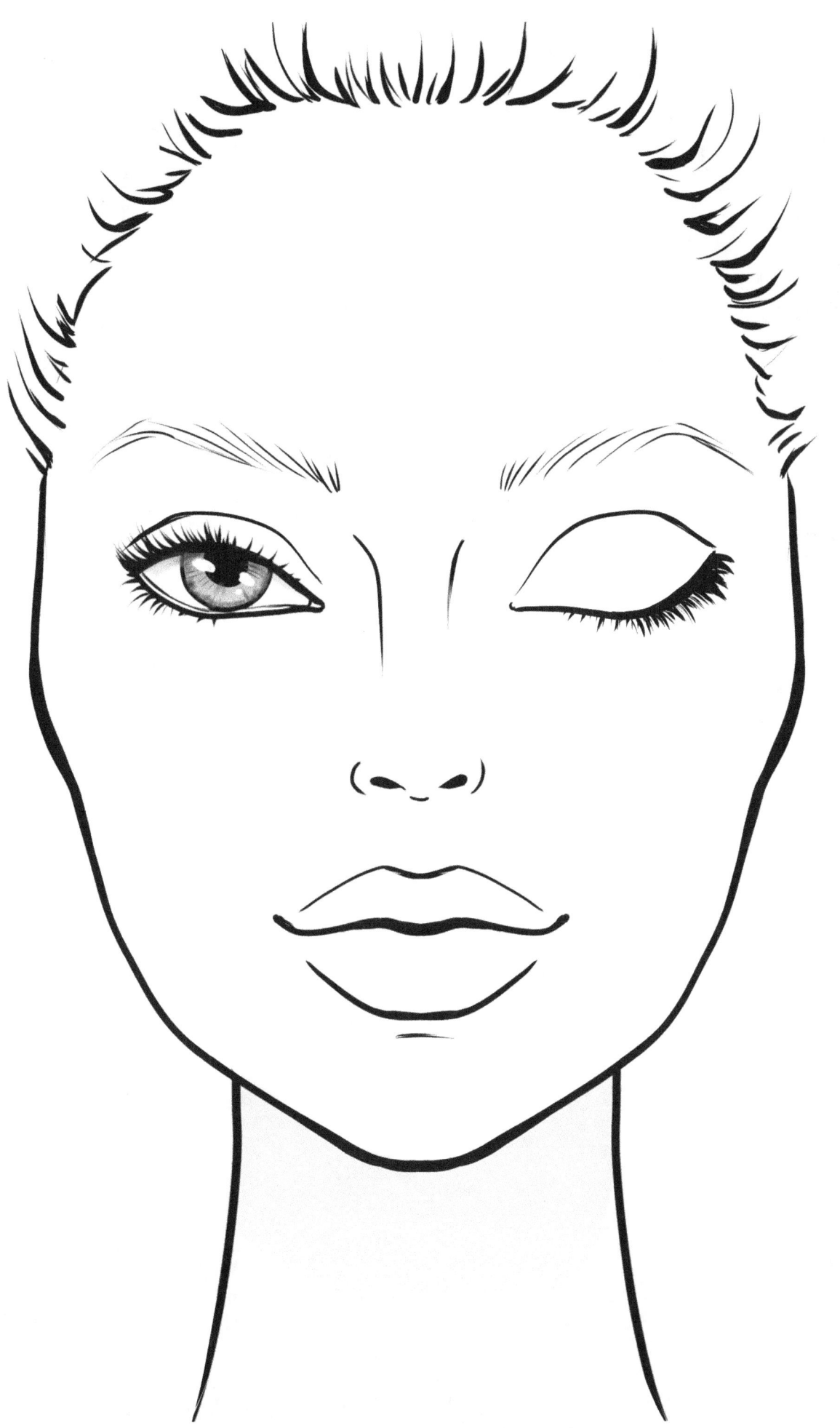

## PREPARATION

Cleanser

-------------------------------------------

Moisturizer

-------------------------------------------

Primer

-------------------------------------------


## FACE

Concealer

-------------------------------------------

Foundation

-------------------------------------------

Powder

-------------------------------------------

Highlighter

-------------------------------------------

Contour

-------------------------------------------

Bronzer

-------------------------------------------

Blush

-------------------------------------------


## EYES

Eyeshadow lid

-------------------------------------------

Eyeshadow crease

-------------------------------------------

Eyeliner

-------------------------------------------

Mascara

-------------------------------------------

Lashes

-------------------------------------------

Brows

-------------------------------------------


## LIPS

Lip color

-------------------------------------------

Lip liner

-------------------------------------------

Lip gloss

-------------------------------------------


## OTHER

-------------------------------------------

-------------------------------------------

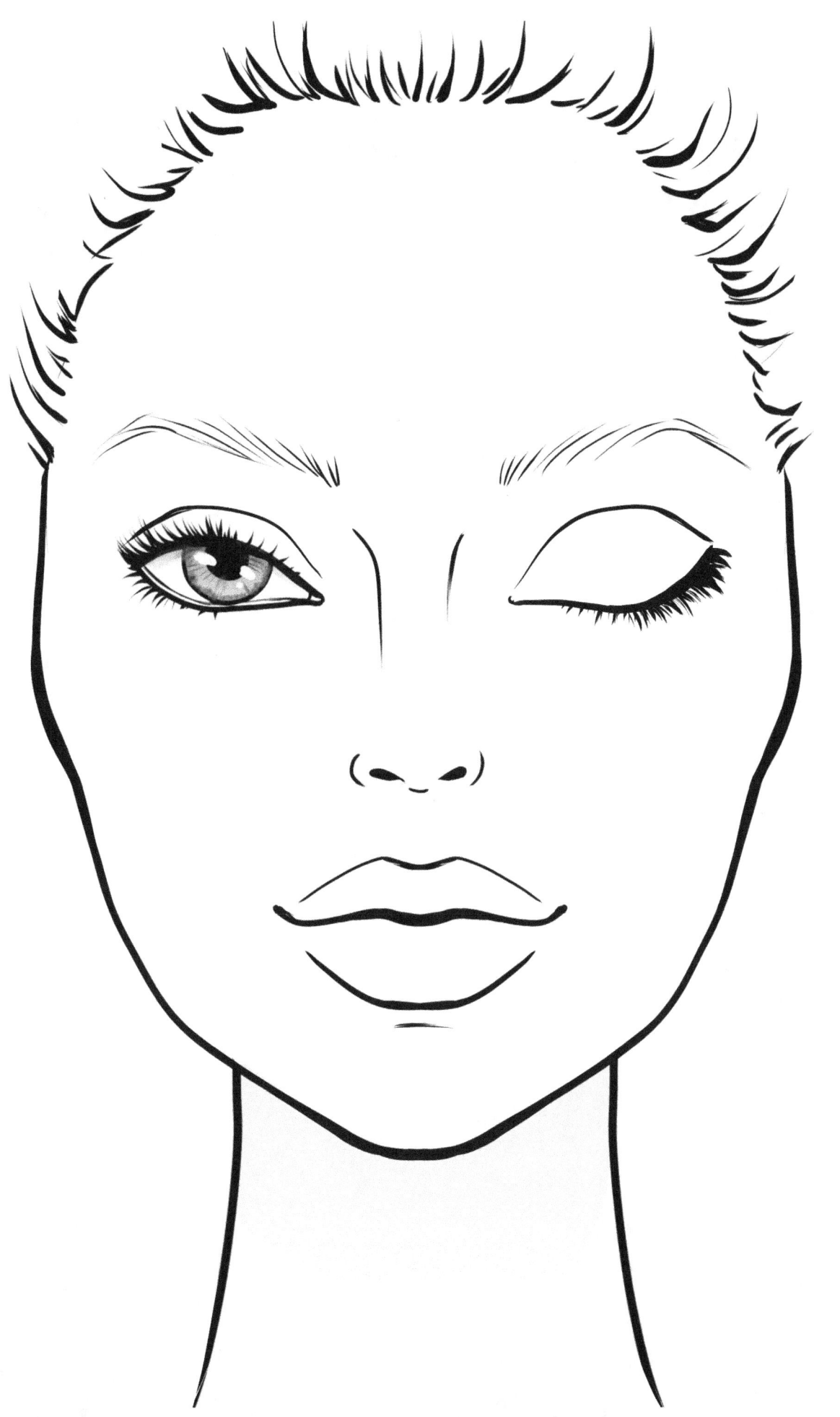

## PREPARATION

Cleanser

---

Moisturizer

---

Primer

---

## FACE

Concealer

---

Foundation

---

Powder

---

Highlighter

---

Contour

---

Bronzer

---

Blush

---

## EYES

Eyeshadow lid

---

Eyeshadow crease

---

Eyeliner

---

Mascara

---

Lashes

---

Brows

---

## LIPS

Lip color

---

Lip liner

---

Lip gloss

---

## OTHER

---

---

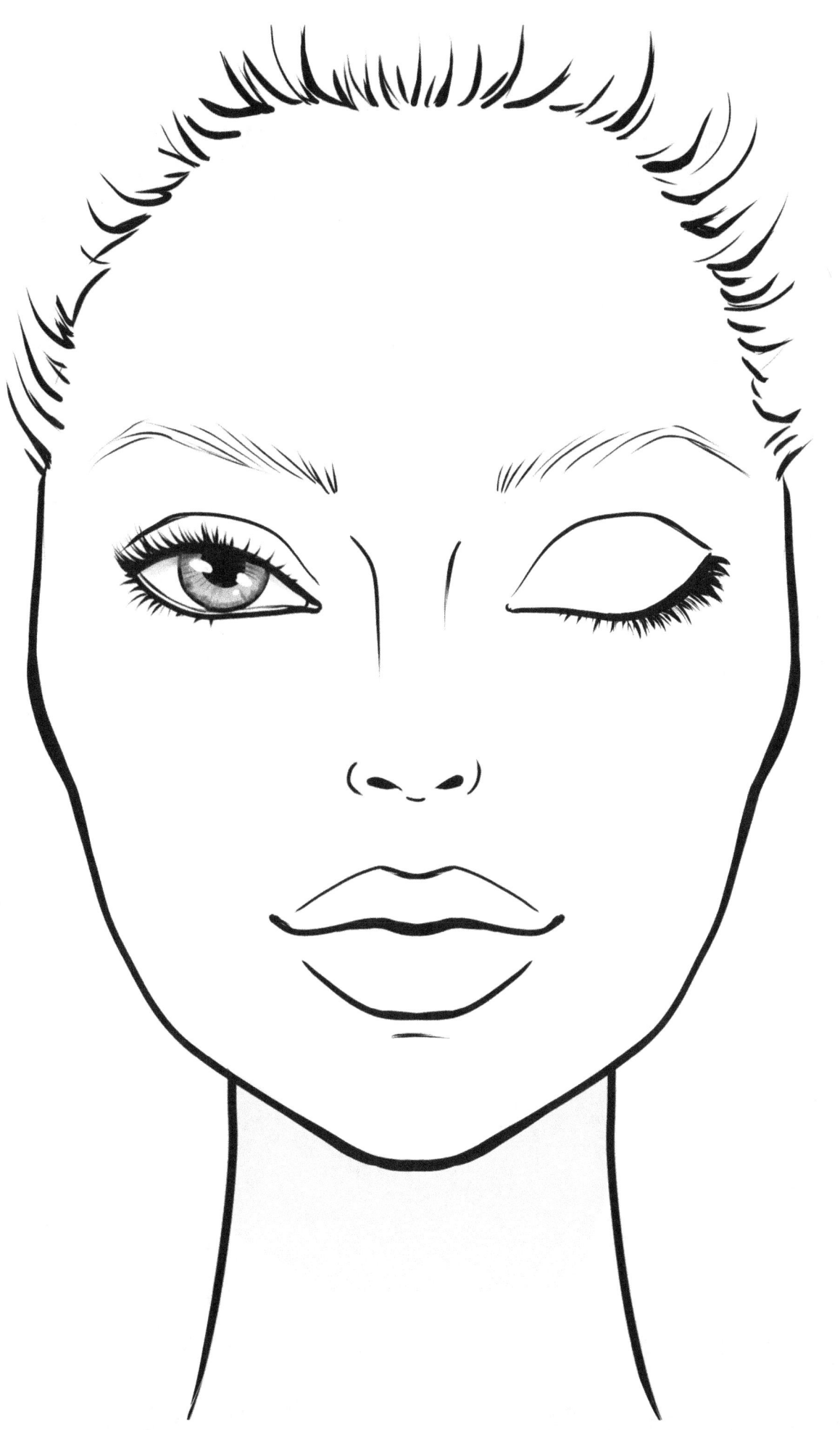

## PREPARATION

Cleanser

-----------------------------------

Moisturizer

-----------------------------------

Primer

-----------------------------------

## FACE

Concealer

-----------------------------------

Foundation

-----------------------------------

Powder

-----------------------------------

Highlighter

-----------------------------------

Contour

-----------------------------------

Bronzer

-----------------------------------

Blush

-----------------------------------

## EYES

Eyeshadow lid

-----------------------------------

Eyeshadow crease

-----------------------------------

Eyeliner

-----------------------------------

Mascara

-----------------------------------

Lashes

-----------------------------------

Brows

-----------------------------------

## LIPS

Lip color

-----------------------------------

Lip liner

-----------------------------------

Lip gloss

-----------------------------------

## OTHER

-----------------------------------

-----------------------------------

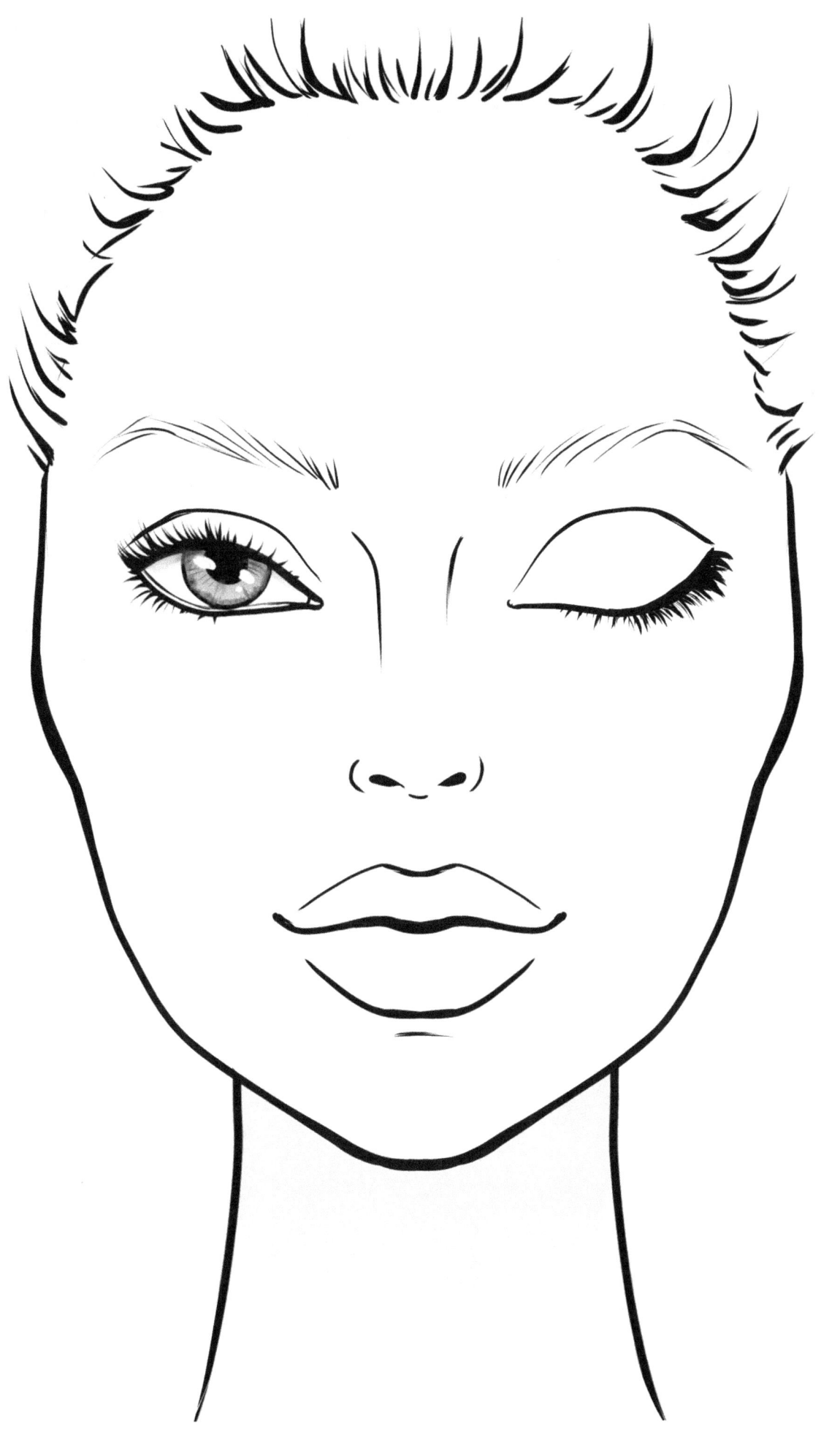

## PREPARATION

Cleanser

---

Moisturizer

---

Primer

---

## FACE

Concealer

---

Foundation

---

Powder

---

Highlighter

---

Contour

---

Bronzer

---

Blush

---

## EYES

Eyeshadow lid

---

Eyeshadow crease

---

Eyeliner

---

Mascara

---

Lashes

---

Brows

---

## LIPS

Lip color

---

Lip liner

---

Lip gloss

---

## OTHER

---

---

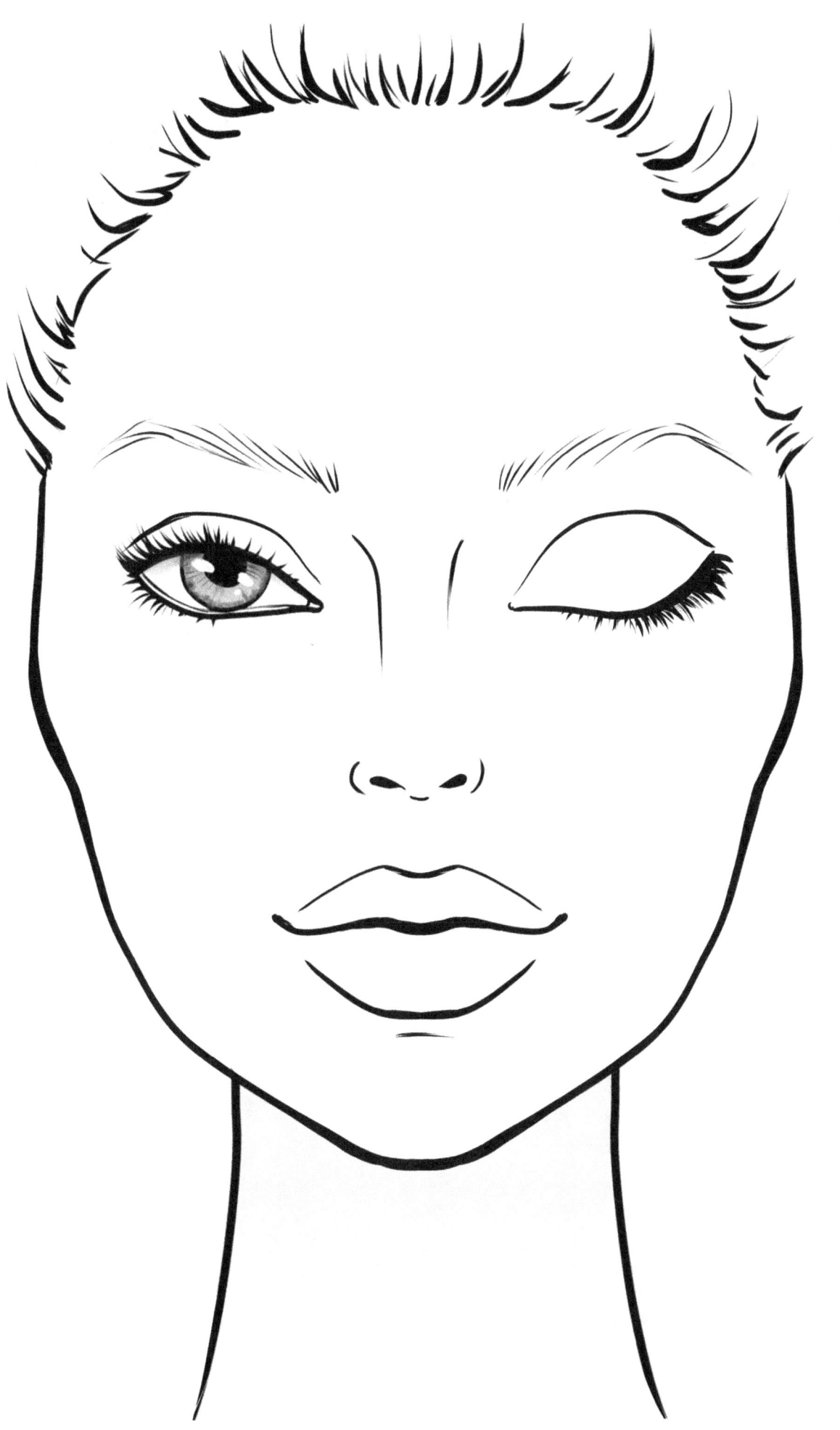

## PREPARATION

Cleanser

---

Moisturizer

---

Primer

---


## FACE

Concealer

---

Foundation

---

Powder

---

Highlighter

---

Contour

---

Bronzer

---

Blush

---


## EYES

Eyeshadow lid

---

Eyeshadow crease

---

Eyeliner

---

Mascara

---

Lashes

---

Brows

---


## LIPS

Lip color

---

Lip liner

---

Lip gloss

---


## OTHER

---

---

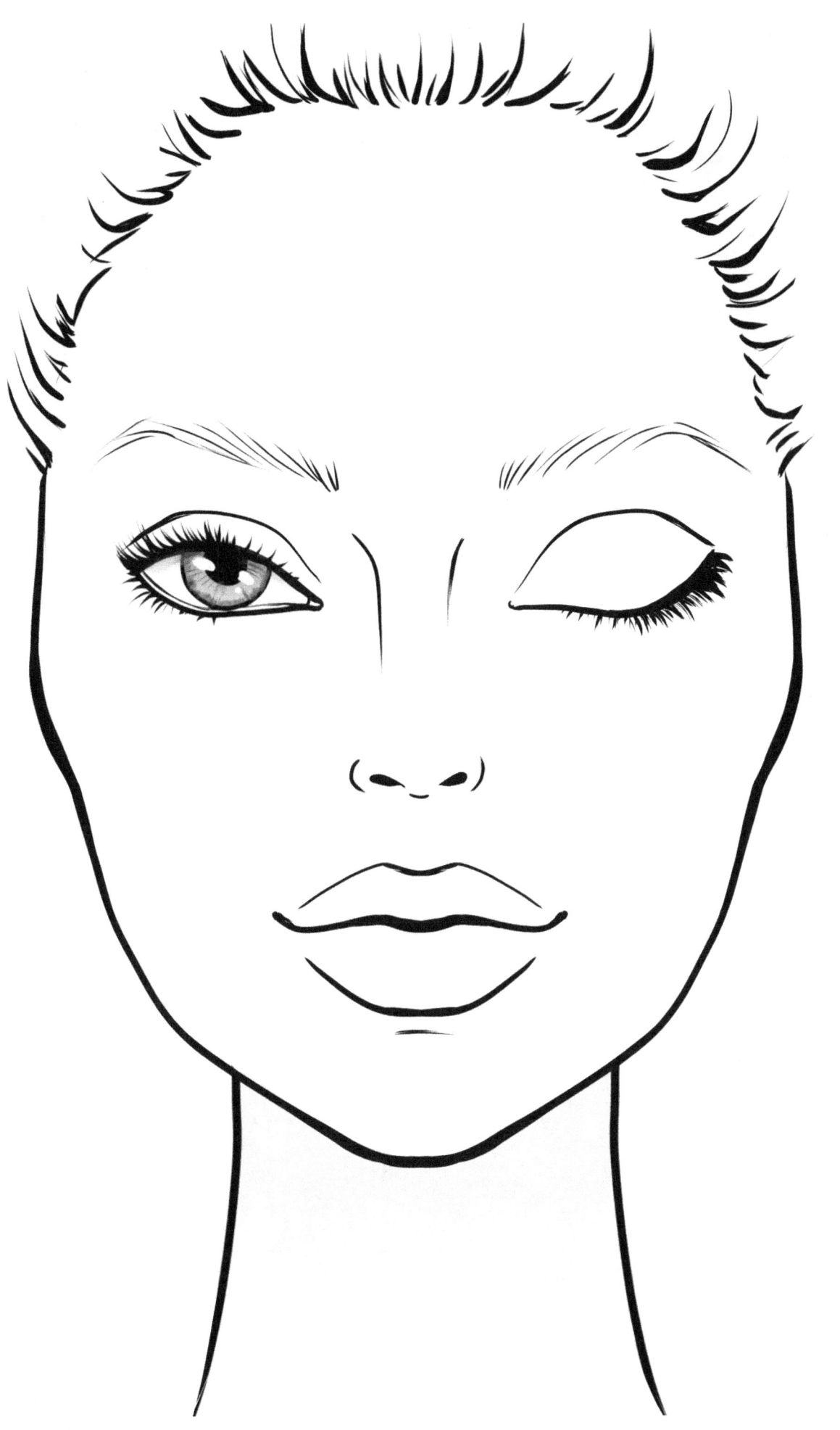

## PREPARATION

Cleanser

----------------------------------------

Moisturizer

----------------------------------------

Primer

----------------------------------------

## FACE

Concealer

----------------------------------------

Foundation

----------------------------------------

Powder

----------------------------------------

Highlighter

----------------------------------------

Contour

----------------------------------------

Bronzer

----------------------------------------

Blush

----------------------------------------

## EYES

Eyeshadow lid

----------------------------------------

Eyeshadow crease

----------------------------------------

Eyeliner

----------------------------------------

Mascara

----------------------------------------

Lashes

----------------------------------------

Brows

----------------------------------------

## LIPS

Lip color

----------------------------------------

Lip liner

----------------------------------------

Lip gloss

----------------------------------------

## OTHER

----------------------------------------

----------------------------------------

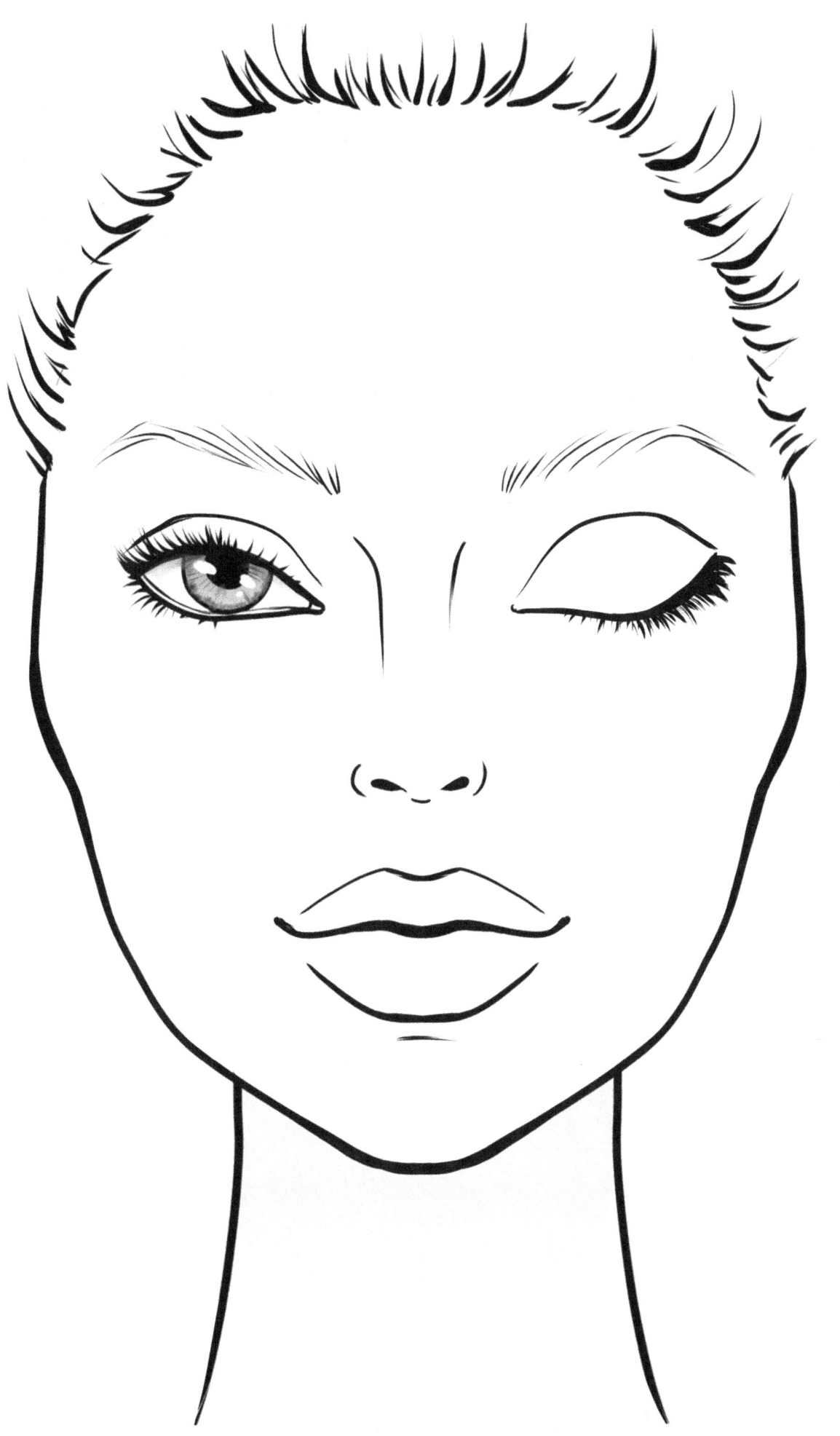

## PREPARATION

Cleanser

--------------------------------------

Moisturizer

--------------------------------------

Primer

--------------------------------------

## FACE

Concealer

--------------------------------------

Foundation

--------------------------------------

Powder

--------------------------------------

Highlighter

--------------------------------------

Contour

--------------------------------------

Bronzer

--------------------------------------

Blush

--------------------------------------

## EYES

Eyeshadow lid

--------------------------------------

Eyeshadow crease

--------------------------------------

Eyeliner

--------------------------------------

Mascara

--------------------------------------

Lashes

--------------------------------------

Brows

--------------------------------------

## LIPS

Lip color

--------------------------------------

Lip liner

--------------------------------------

Lip gloss

--------------------------------------

## OTHER

--------------------------------------

--------------------------------------

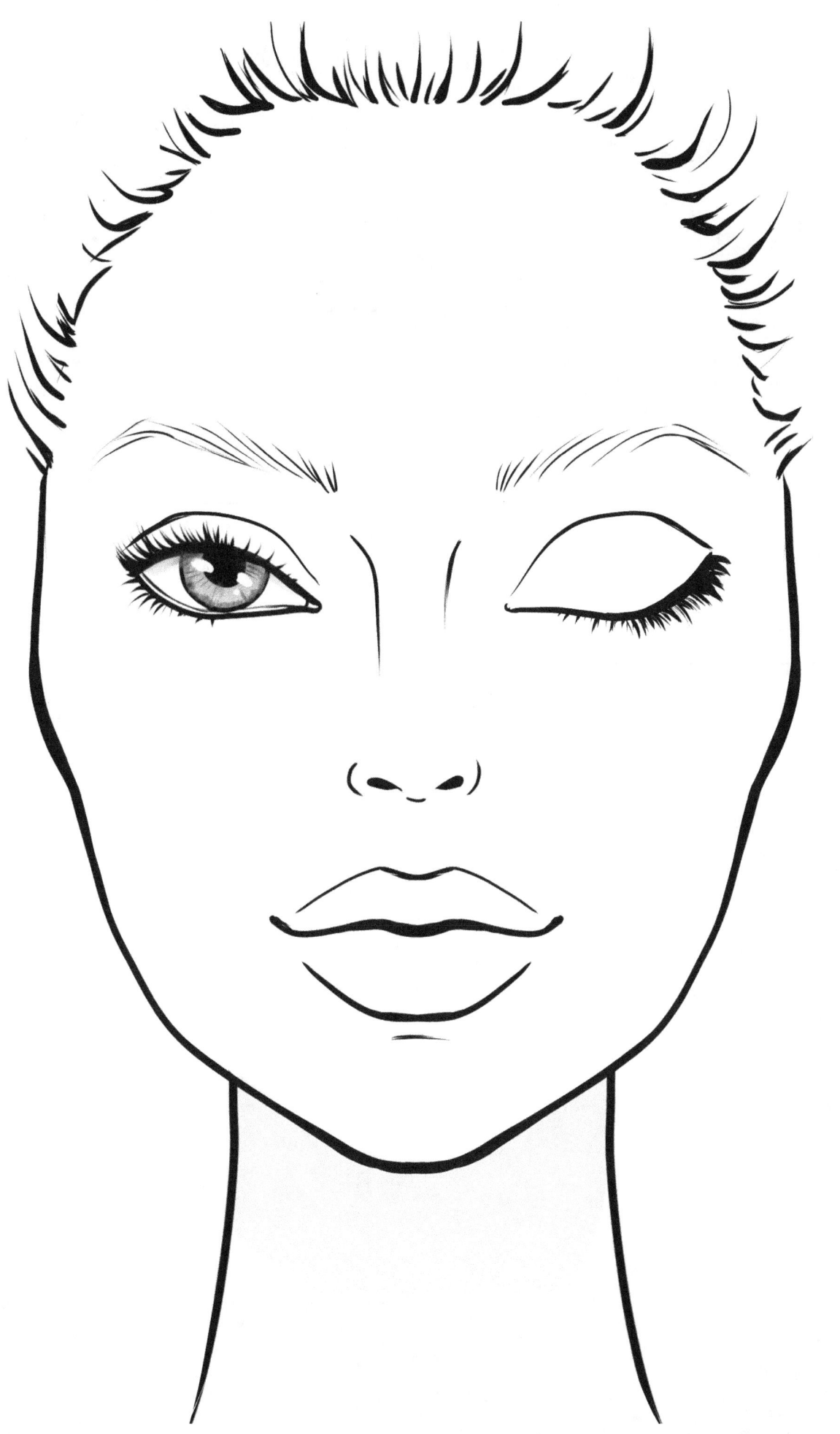

## PREPARATION

Cleanser

-------------------------------------------

Moisturizer

-------------------------------------------

Primer

-------------------------------------------

## FACE

Concealer

-------------------------------------------

Foundation

-------------------------------------------

Powder

-------------------------------------------

Highlighter

-------------------------------------------

Contour

-------------------------------------------

Bronzer

-------------------------------------------

Blush

-------------------------------------------

## EYES

Eyeshadow lid

-------------------------------------------

Eyeshadow crease

-------------------------------------------

Eyeliner

-------------------------------------------

Mascara

-------------------------------------------

Lashes

-------------------------------------------

Brows

-------------------------------------------

## LIPS

Lip color

-------------------------------------------

Lip liner

-------------------------------------------

Lip gloss

-------------------------------------------

## OTHER

-------------------------------------------

-------------------------------------------

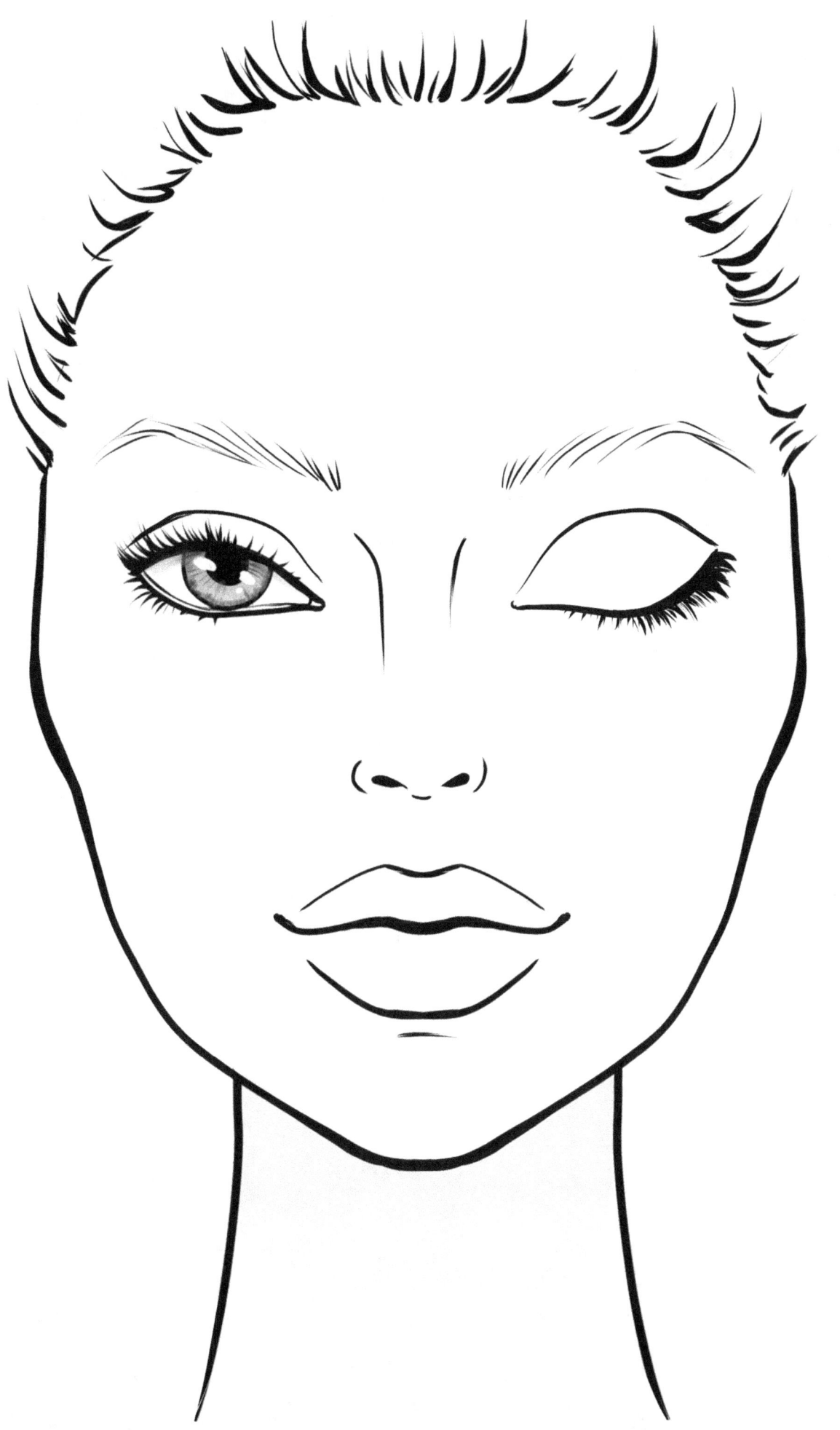

## PREPARATION

Cleanser

---

Moisturizer

---

Primer

---

## FACE

Concealer

---

Foundation

---

Powder

---

Highlighter

---

Contour

---

Bronzer

---

Blush

---

## EYES

Eyeshadow lid

---

Eyeshadow crease

---

Eyeliner

---

Mascara

---

Lashes

---

Brows

---

## LIPS

Lip color

---

Lip liner

---

Lip gloss

---

## OTHER

---

---

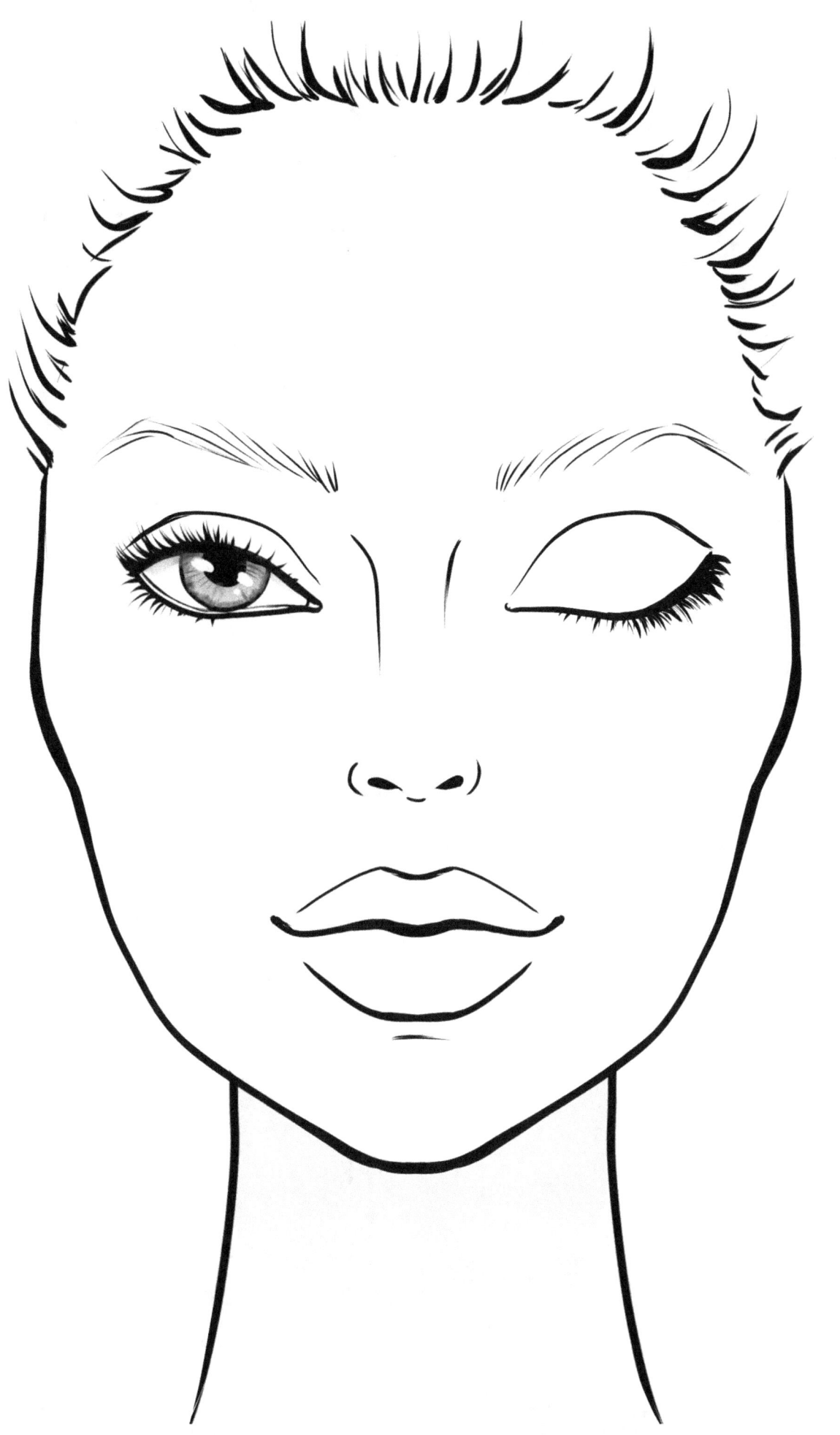

## PREPARATION

Cleanser

-------------------------------------------

Moisturizer

-------------------------------------------

Primer

-------------------------------------------

## FACE

Concealer

-------------------------------------------

Foundation

-------------------------------------------

Powder

-------------------------------------------

Highlighter

-------------------------------------------

Contour

-------------------------------------------

Bronzer

-------------------------------------------

Blush

-------------------------------------------

## EYES

Eyeshadow lid

-------------------------------------------

Eyeshadow crease

-------------------------------------------

Eyeliner

-------------------------------------------

Mascara

-------------------------------------------

Lashes

-------------------------------------------

Brows

-------------------------------------------

## LIPS

Lip color

-------------------------------------------

Lip liner

-------------------------------------------

Lip gloss

-------------------------------------------

## OTHER

-------------------------------------------

-------------------------------------------

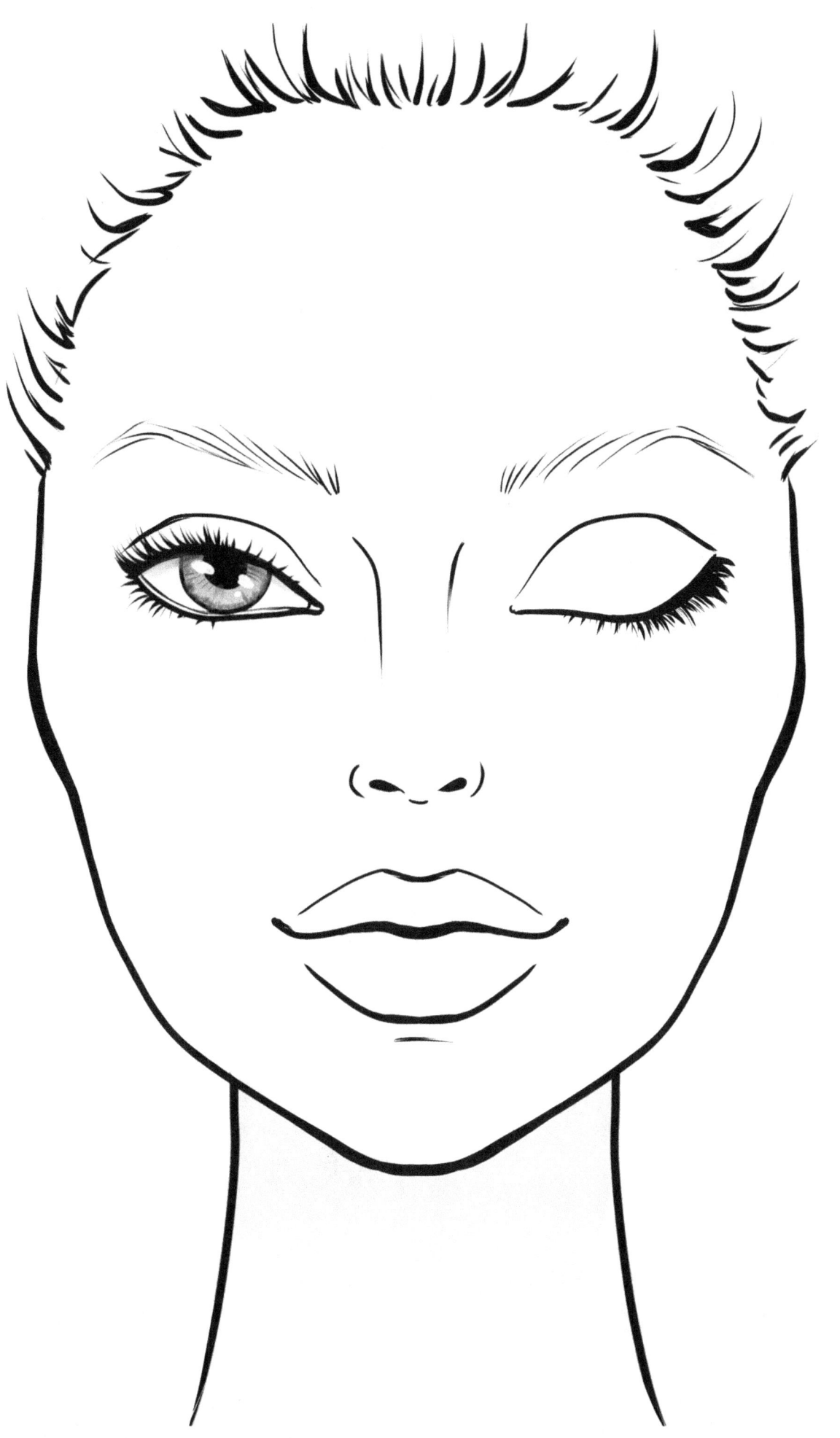

## PREPARATION

Cleanser

------------------------------------

Moisturizer

------------------------------------

Primer

------------------------------------

## FACE

Concealer

------------------------------------

Foundation

------------------------------------

Powder

------------------------------------

Highlighter

------------------------------------

Contour

------------------------------------

Bronzer

------------------------------------

Blush

------------------------------------

## EYES

Eyeshadow lid

------------------------------------

Eyeshadow crease

------------------------------------

Eyeliner

------------------------------------

Mascara

------------------------------------

Lashes

------------------------------------

Brows

------------------------------------

## LIPS

Lip color

------------------------------------

Lip liner

------------------------------------

Lip gloss

------------------------------------

## OTHER

------------------------------------

------------------------------------

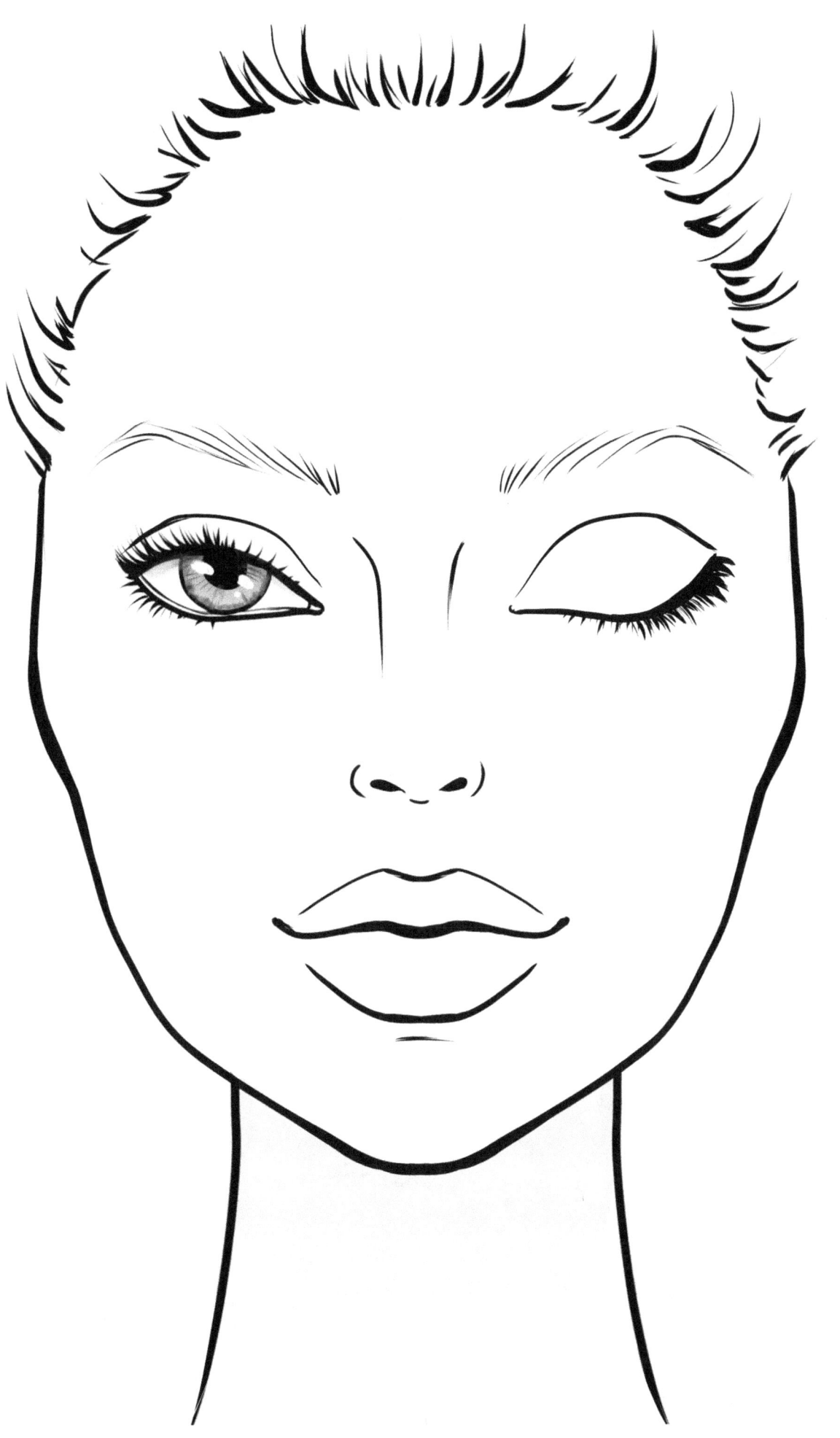

## PREPARATION

Cleanser

------------------------------

Moisturizer

------------------------------

Primer

------------------------------

## FACE

Concealer

------------------------------

Foundation

------------------------------

Powder

------------------------------

Highlighter

------------------------------

Contour

------------------------------

Bronzer

------------------------------

Blush

------------------------------

## EYES

Eyeshadow lid

------------------------------

Eyeshadow crease

------------------------------

Eyeliner

------------------------------

Mascara

------------------------------

Lashes

------------------------------

Brows

------------------------------

## LIPS

Lip color

------------------------------

Lip liner

------------------------------

Lip gloss

------------------------------

## OTHER

------------------------------

------------------------------

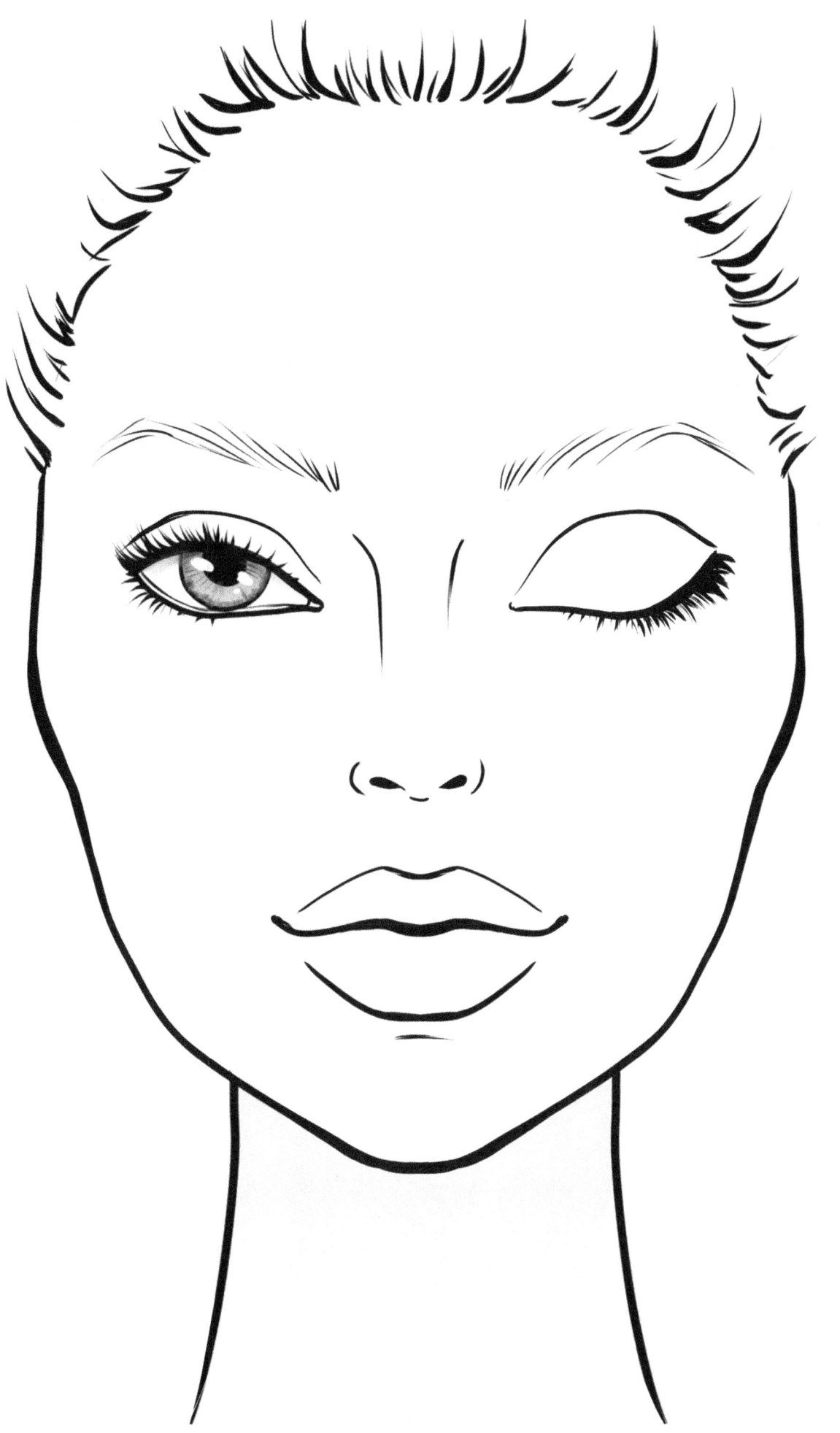

## PREPARATION

Cleanser

------------------------------------------------

Moisturizer

------------------------------------------------

Primer

------------------------------------------------

## FACE

Concealer

------------------------------------------------

Foundation

------------------------------------------------

Powder

------------------------------------------------

Highlighter

------------------------------------------------

Contour

------------------------------------------------

Bronzer

------------------------------------------------

Blush

------------------------------------------------

## EYES

Eyeshadow lid

------------------------------------------------

Eyeshadow crease

------------------------------------------------

Eyeliner

------------------------------------------------

Mascara

------------------------------------------------

Lashes

------------------------------------------------

Brows

------------------------------------------------

## LIPS

Lip color

------------------------------------------------

Lip liner

------------------------------------------------

Lip gloss

------------------------------------------------

## OTHER

------------------------------------------------

------------------------------------------------

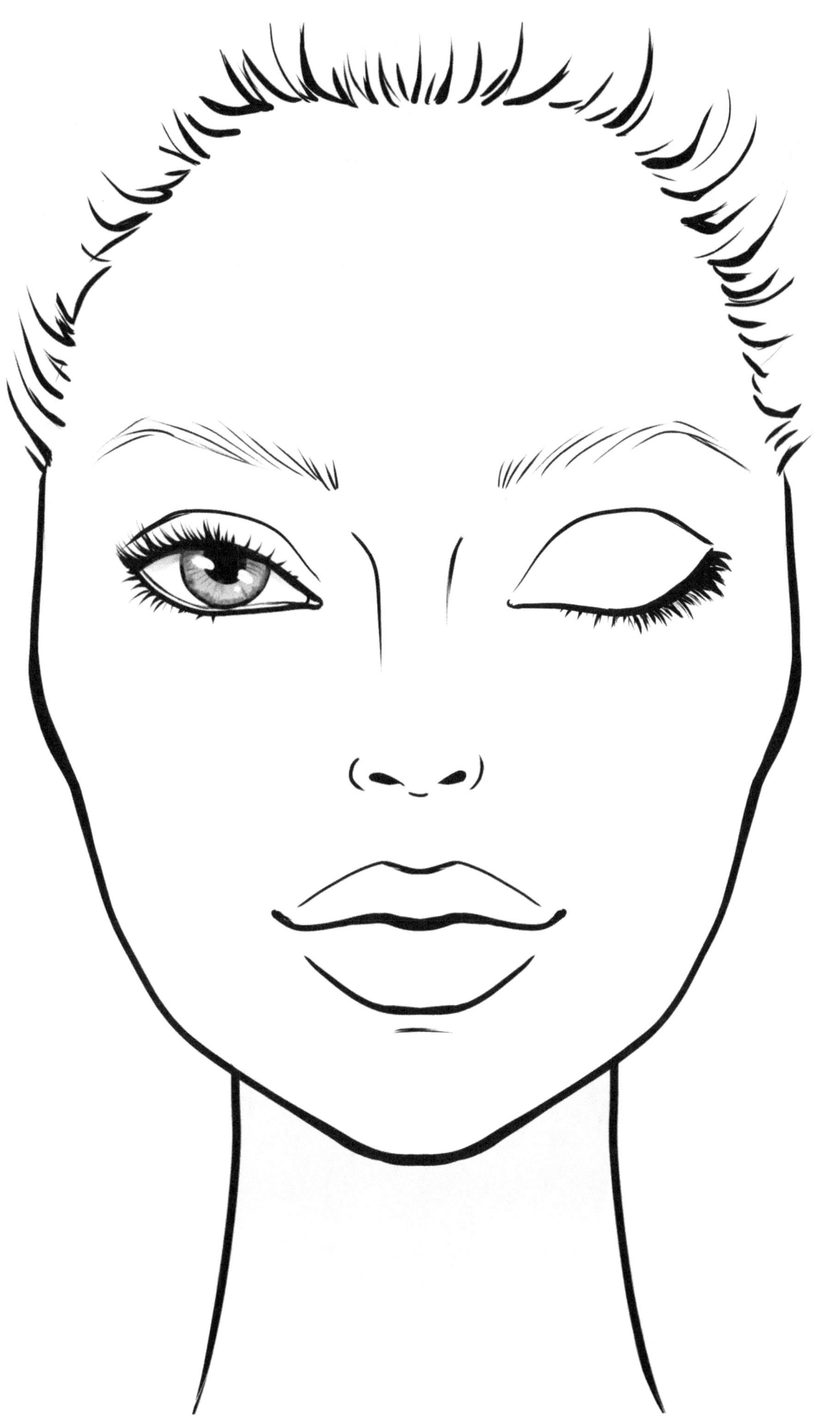

## PREPARATION

Cleanser

------------------------------------------------

Moisturizer

------------------------------------------------

Primer

------------------------------------------------

## FACE

Concealer

------------------------------------------------

Foundation

------------------------------------------------

Powder

------------------------------------------------

Highlighter

------------------------------------------------

Contour

------------------------------------------------

Bronzer

------------------------------------------------

Blush

------------------------------------------------

## EYES

Eyeshadow lid

------------------------------------------------

Eyeshadow crease

------------------------------------------------

Eyeliner

------------------------------------------------

Mascara

------------------------------------------------

Lashes

------------------------------------------------

Brows

------------------------------------------------

## LIPS

Lip color

------------------------------------------------

Lip liner

------------------------------------------------

Lip gloss

------------------------------------------------

## OTHER

------------------------------------------------

------------------------------------------------

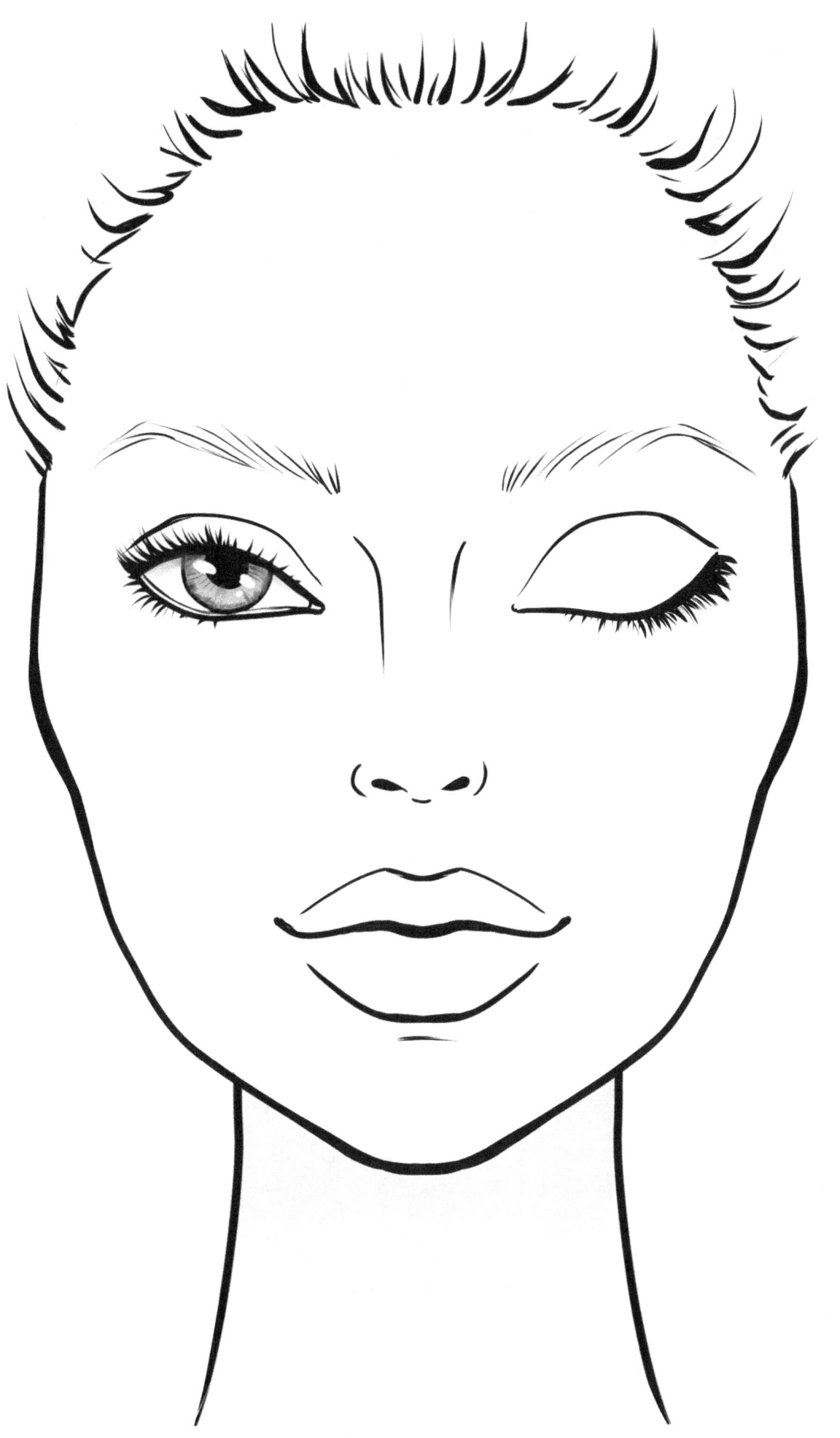

## PREPARATION

Cleanser

----------------------------------------

Moisturizer

----------------------------------------

Primer

----------------------------------------

## FACE

Concealer

----------------------------------------

Foundation

----------------------------------------

Powder

----------------------------------------

Highlighter

----------------------------------------

Contour

----------------------------------------

Bronzer

----------------------------------------

Blush

----------------------------------------

## EYES

Eyeshadow lid

----------------------------------------

Eyeshadow crease

----------------------------------------

Eyeliner

----------------------------------------

Mascara

----------------------------------------

Lashes

----------------------------------------

Brows

----------------------------------------

## LIPS

Lip color

----------------------------------------

Lip liner

----------------------------------------

Lip gloss

----------------------------------------

## OTHER

----------------------------------------

----------------------------------------

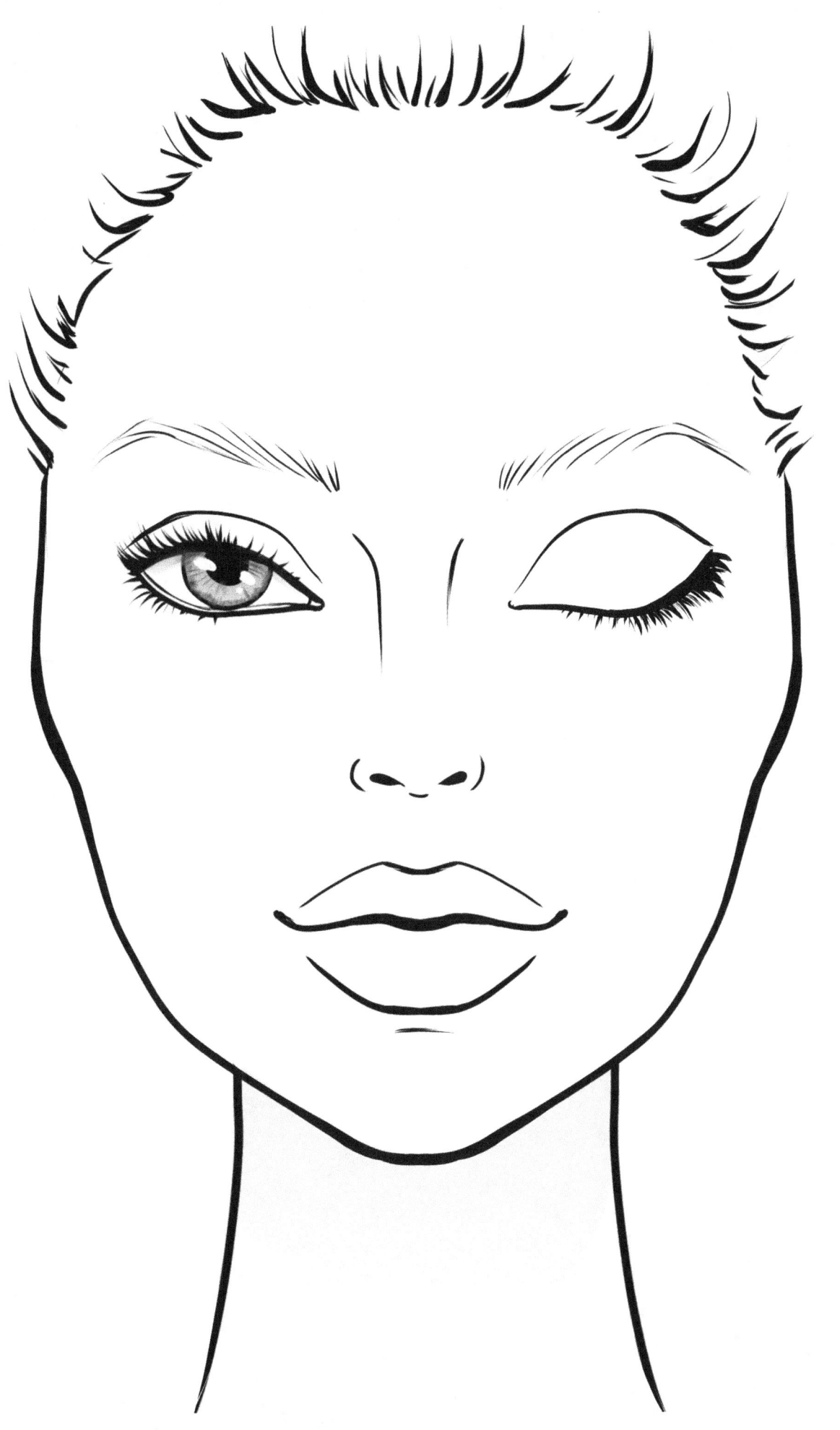

## PREPARATION

Cleanser

----------------------------------------

Moisturizer

----------------------------------------

Primer

----------------------------------------

## FACE

Concealer

----------------------------------------

Foundation

----------------------------------------

Powder

----------------------------------------

Highlighter

----------------------------------------

Contour

----------------------------------------

Bronzer

----------------------------------------

Blush

----------------------------------------

## EYES

Eyeshadow lid

----------------------------------------

Eyeshadow crease

----------------------------------------

Eyeliner

----------------------------------------

Mascara

----------------------------------------

Lashes

----------------------------------------

Brows

----------------------------------------

## LIPS

Lip color

----------------------------------------

Lip liner

----------------------------------------

Lip gloss

----------------------------------------

## OTHER

----------------------------------------

----------------------------------------

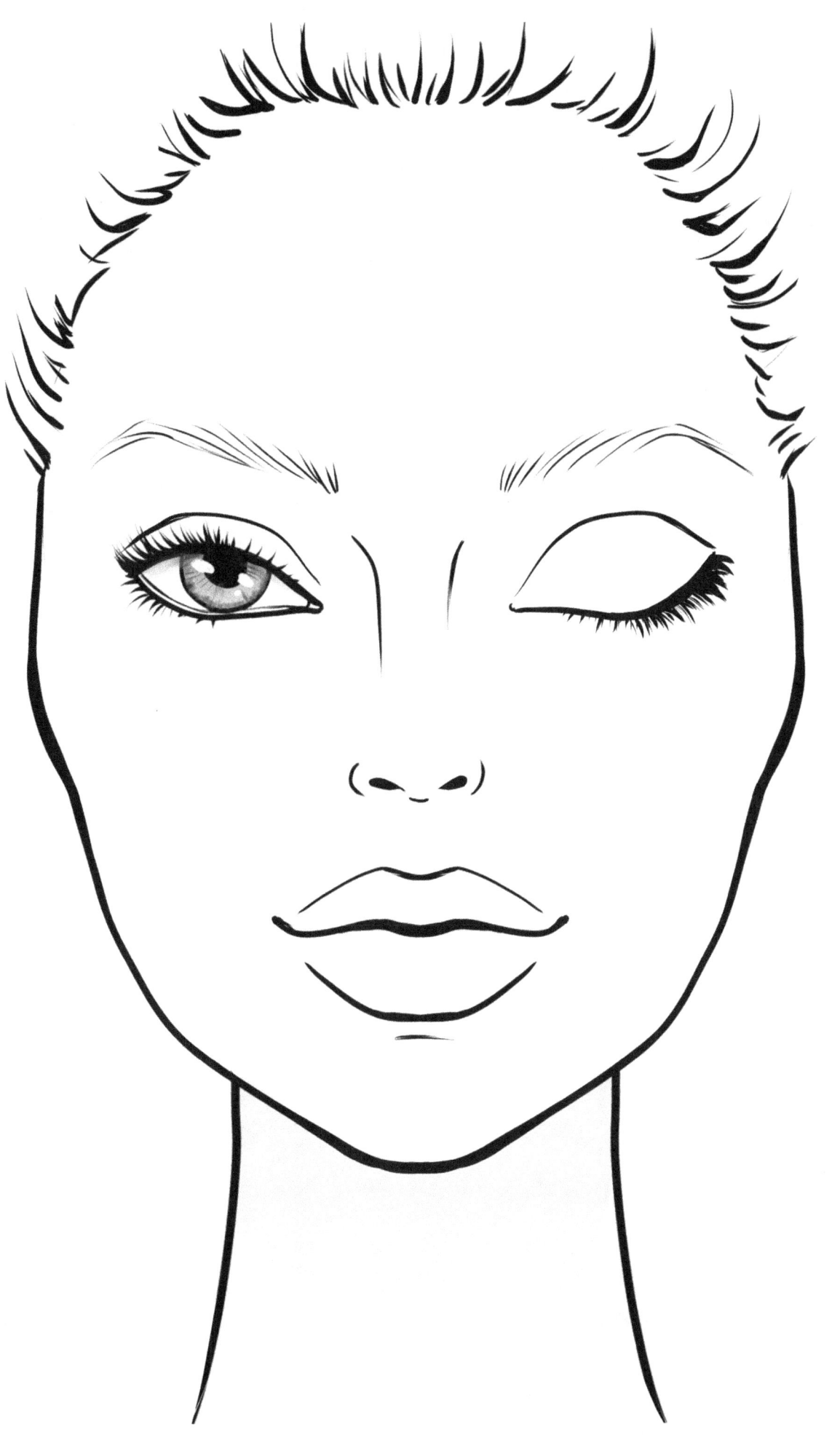

# CLOSED EYES
# FACE CHARTS

## PREPARATION

Cleanser
-------------------------------------

Moisturizer
-------------------------------------

Primer
-------------------------------------

## FACE

Concealer
-------------------------------------

Foundation
-------------------------------------

Powder
-------------------------------------

Highlighter
-------------------------------------

Contour
-------------------------------------

Bronzer
-------------------------------------

Blush
-------------------------------------

## EYES

Eyeshadow lid
-------------------------------------

Eyeshadow crease
-------------------------------------

Eyeliner
-------------------------------------

Mascara
-------------------------------------

Lashes
-------------------------------------

Brows
-------------------------------------

## LIPS

Lip color
-------------------------------------

Lip liner
-------------------------------------

Lip gloss
-------------------------------------

## OTHER

-------------------------------------

-------------------------------------

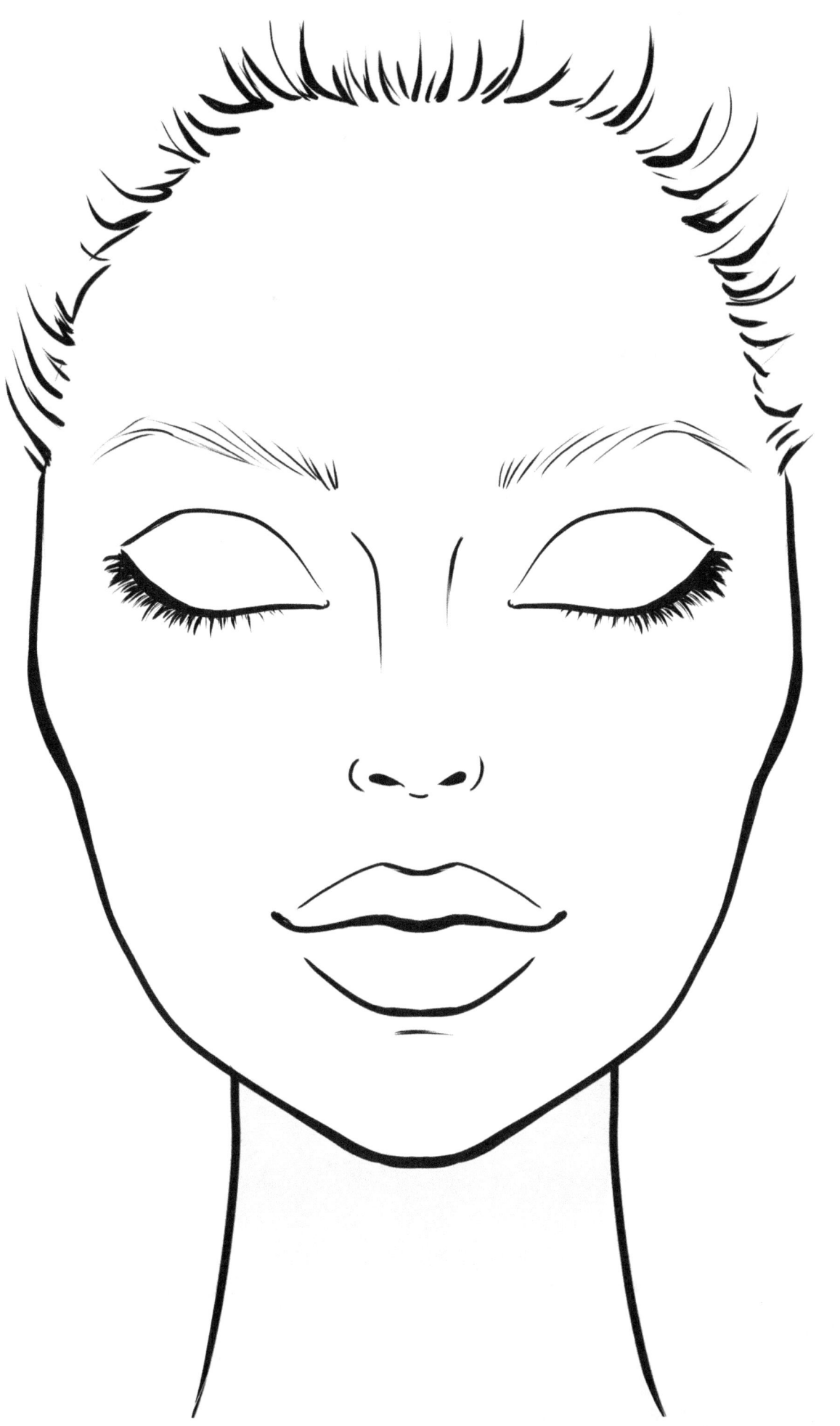

## PREPARATION

Cleanser

------------------------------

Moisturizer

------------------------------

Primer

------------------------------

## FACE

Concealer

------------------------------

Foundation

------------------------------

Powder

------------------------------

Highlighter

------------------------------

Contour

------------------------------

Bronzer

------------------------------

Blush

------------------------------

## EYES

Eyeshadow lid

------------------------------

Eyeshadow crease

------------------------------

Eyeliner

------------------------------

Mascara

------------------------------

Lashes

------------------------------

Brows

------------------------------

## LIPS

Lip color

------------------------------

Lip liner

------------------------------

Lip gloss

------------------------------

## OTHER

------------------------------

------------------------------

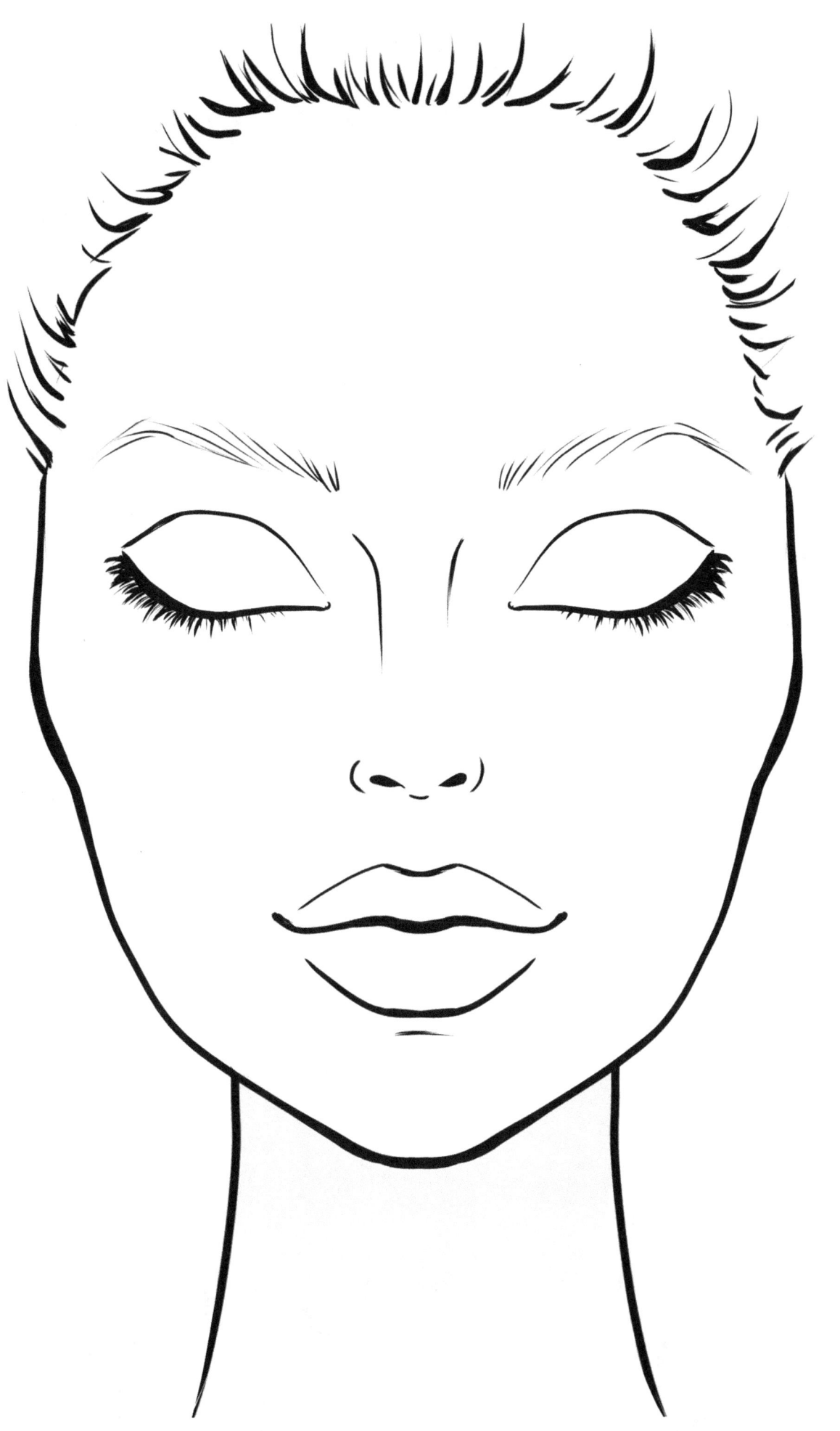

## PREPARATION

Cleanser

----------------------------------------

Moisturizer

----------------------------------------

Primer

----------------------------------------

## FACE

Concealer

----------------------------------------

Foundation

----------------------------------------

Powder

----------------------------------------

Highlighter

----------------------------------------

Contour

----------------------------------------

Bronzer

----------------------------------------

Blush

----------------------------------------

## EYES

Eyeshadow lid

----------------------------------------

Eyeshadow crease

----------------------------------------

Eyeliner

----------------------------------------

Mascara

----------------------------------------

Lashes

----------------------------------------

Brows

----------------------------------------

## LIPS

Lip color

----------------------------------------

Lip liner

----------------------------------------

Lip gloss

----------------------------------------

## OTHER

----------------------------------------

----------------------------------------

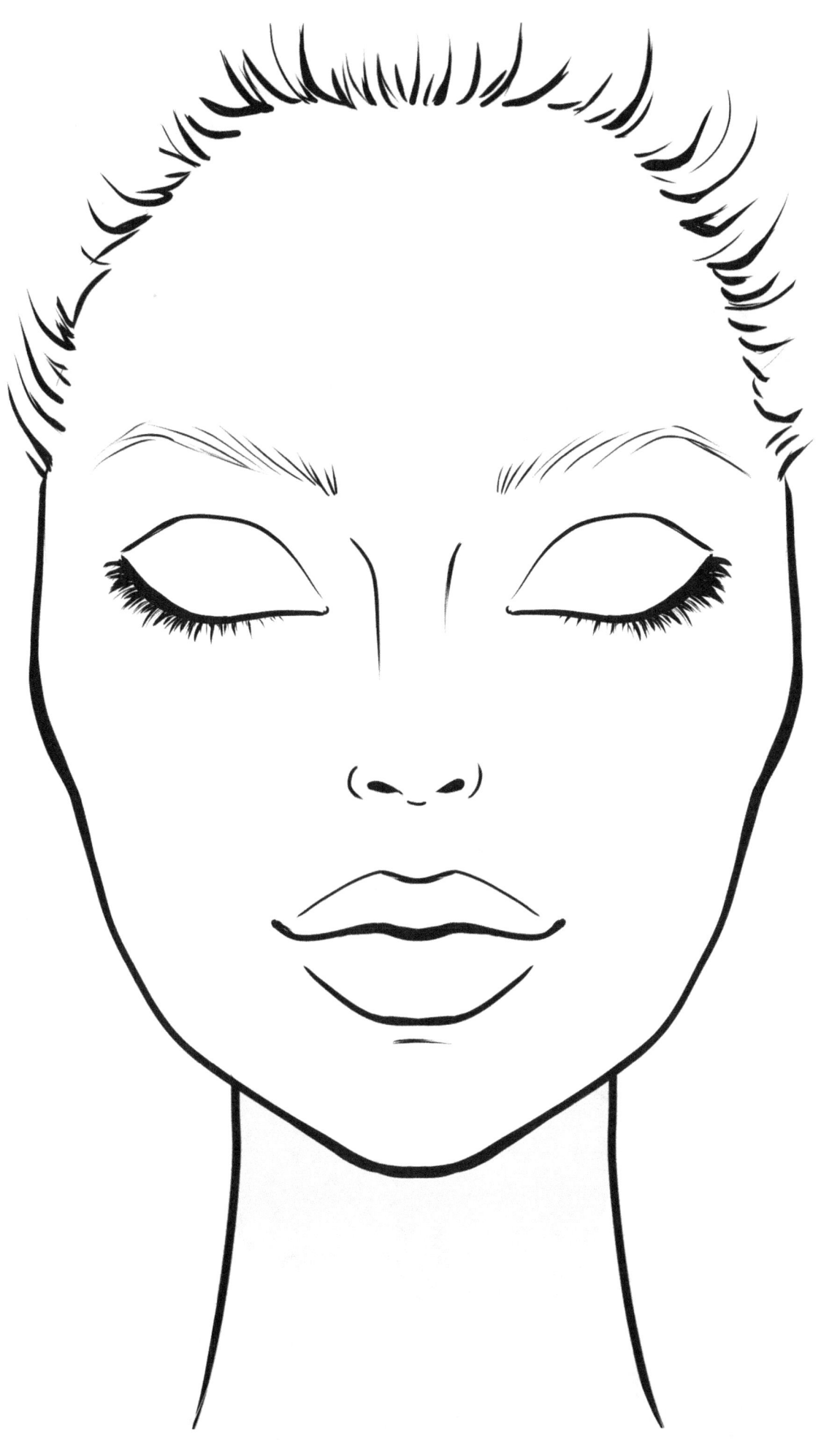

## PREPARATION

Cleanser

------------------------------------

Moisturizer

------------------------------------

Primer

------------------------------------

## FACE

Concealer

------------------------------------

Foundation

------------------------------------

Powder

------------------------------------

Highlighter

------------------------------------

Contour

------------------------------------

Bronzer

------------------------------------

Blush

------------------------------------

## EYES

Eyeshadow lid

------------------------------------

Eyeshadow crease

------------------------------------

Eyeliner

------------------------------------

Mascara

------------------------------------

Lashes

------------------------------------

Brows

------------------------------------

## LIPS

Lip color

------------------------------------

Lip liner

------------------------------------

Lip gloss

------------------------------------

## OTHER

------------------------------------

------------------------------------

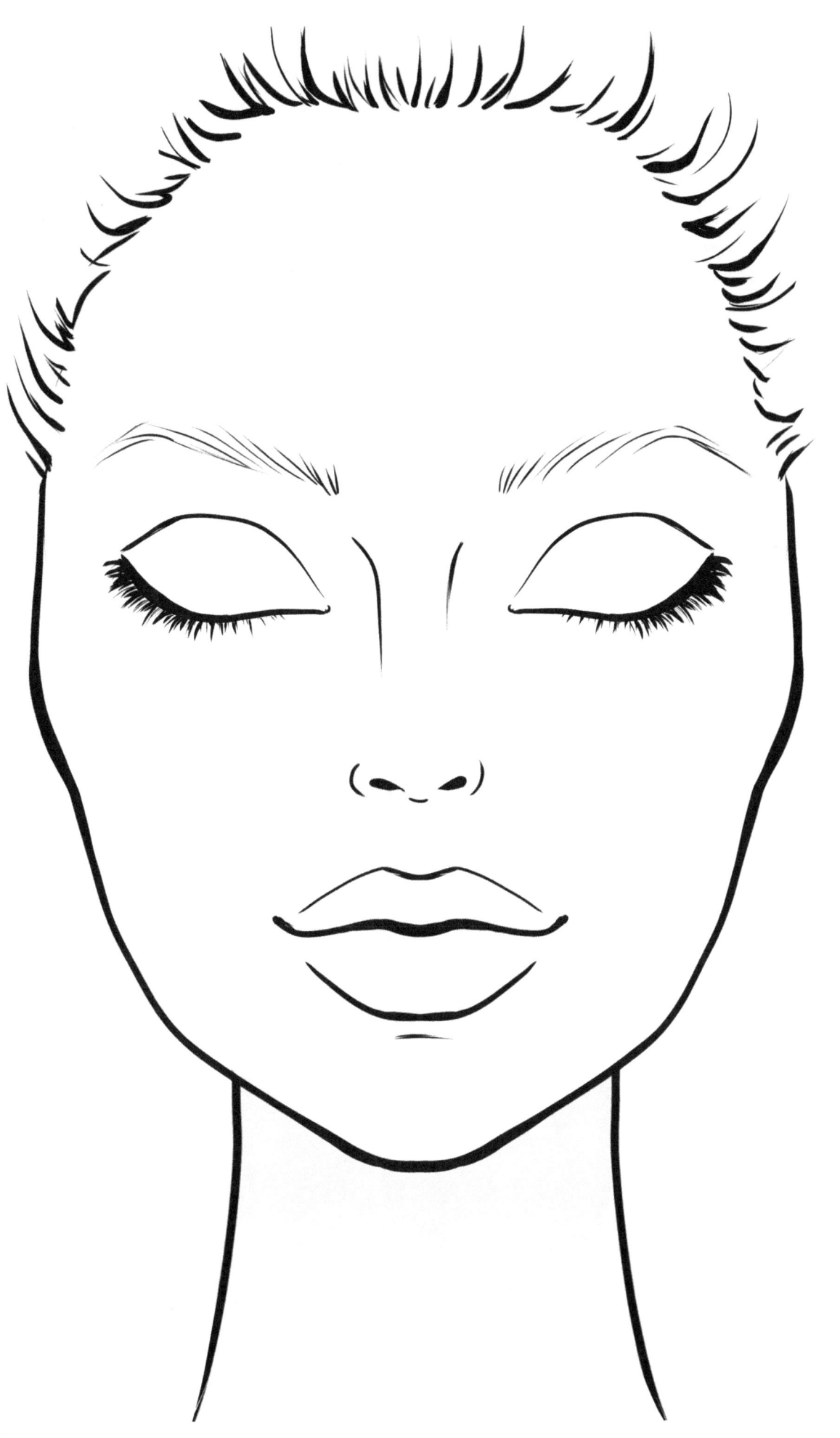

## PREPARATION

Cleanser

----------------------------------------

Moisturizer

----------------------------------------

Primer

----------------------------------------

## FACE

Concealer

----------------------------------------

Foundation

----------------------------------------

Powder

----------------------------------------

Highlighter

----------------------------------------

Contour

----------------------------------------

Bronzer

----------------------------------------

Blush

----------------------------------------

## EYES

Eyeshadow lid

----------------------------------------

Eyeshadow crease

----------------------------------------

Eyeliner

----------------------------------------

Mascara

----------------------------------------

Lashes

----------------------------------------

Brows

----------------------------------------

## LIPS

Lip color

----------------------------------------

Lip liner

----------------------------------------

Lip gloss

----------------------------------------

## OTHER

----------------------------------------

----------------------------------------

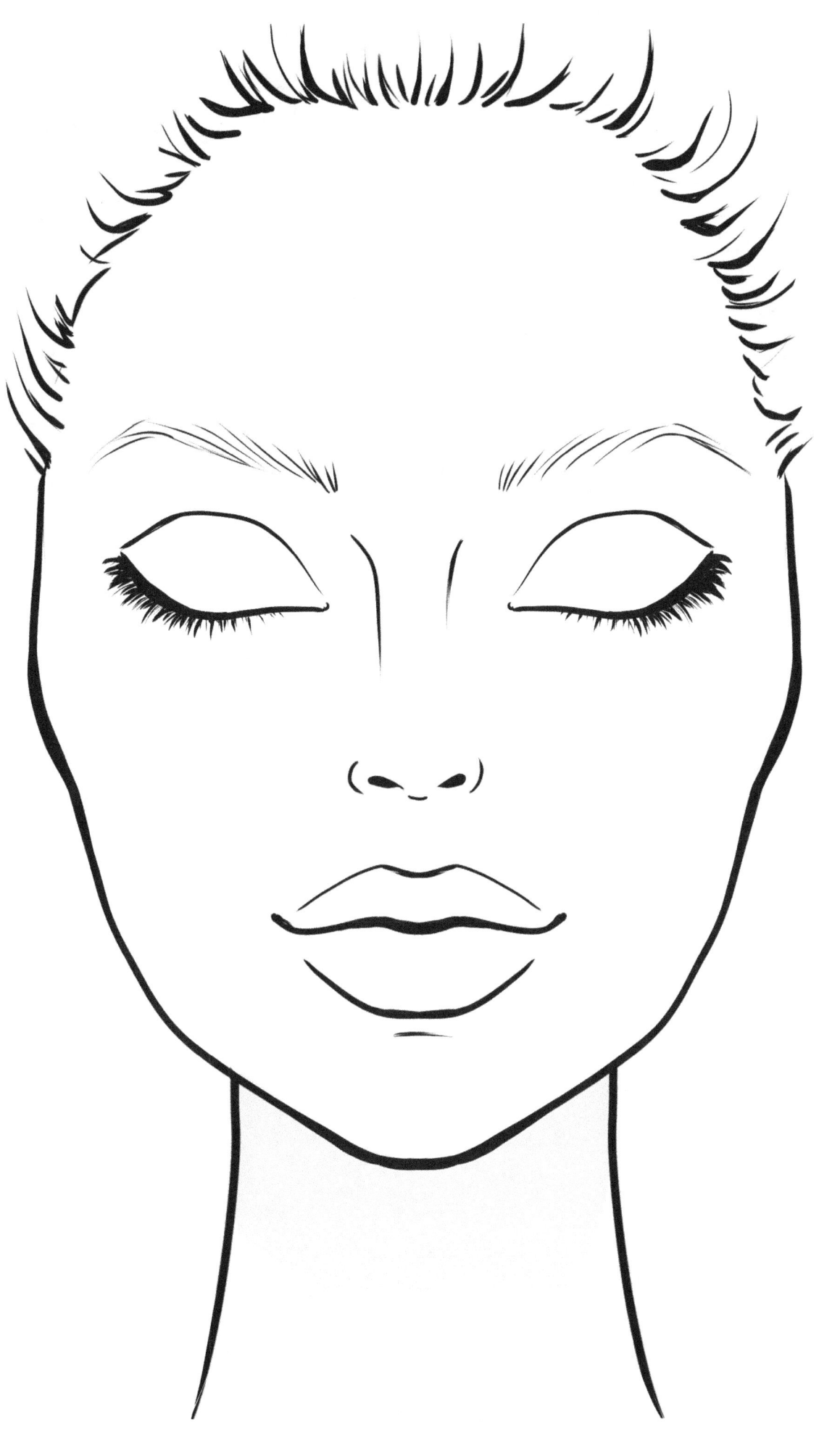

## PREPARATION

Cleanser

-------------------------------------

Moisturizer

-------------------------------------

Primer

-------------------------------------


## FACE

Concealer

-------------------------------------

Foundation

-------------------------------------

Powder

-------------------------------------

Highlighter

-------------------------------------

Contour

-------------------------------------

Bronzer

-------------------------------------

Blush

-------------------------------------


## EYES

Eyeshadow lid

-------------------------------------

Eyeshadow crease

-------------------------------------

Eyeliner

-------------------------------------

Mascara

-------------------------------------

Lashes

-------------------------------------

Brows

-------------------------------------


## LIPS

Lip color

-------------------------------------

Lip liner

-------------------------------------

Lip gloss

-------------------------------------


## OTHER

-------------------------------------

-------------------------------------

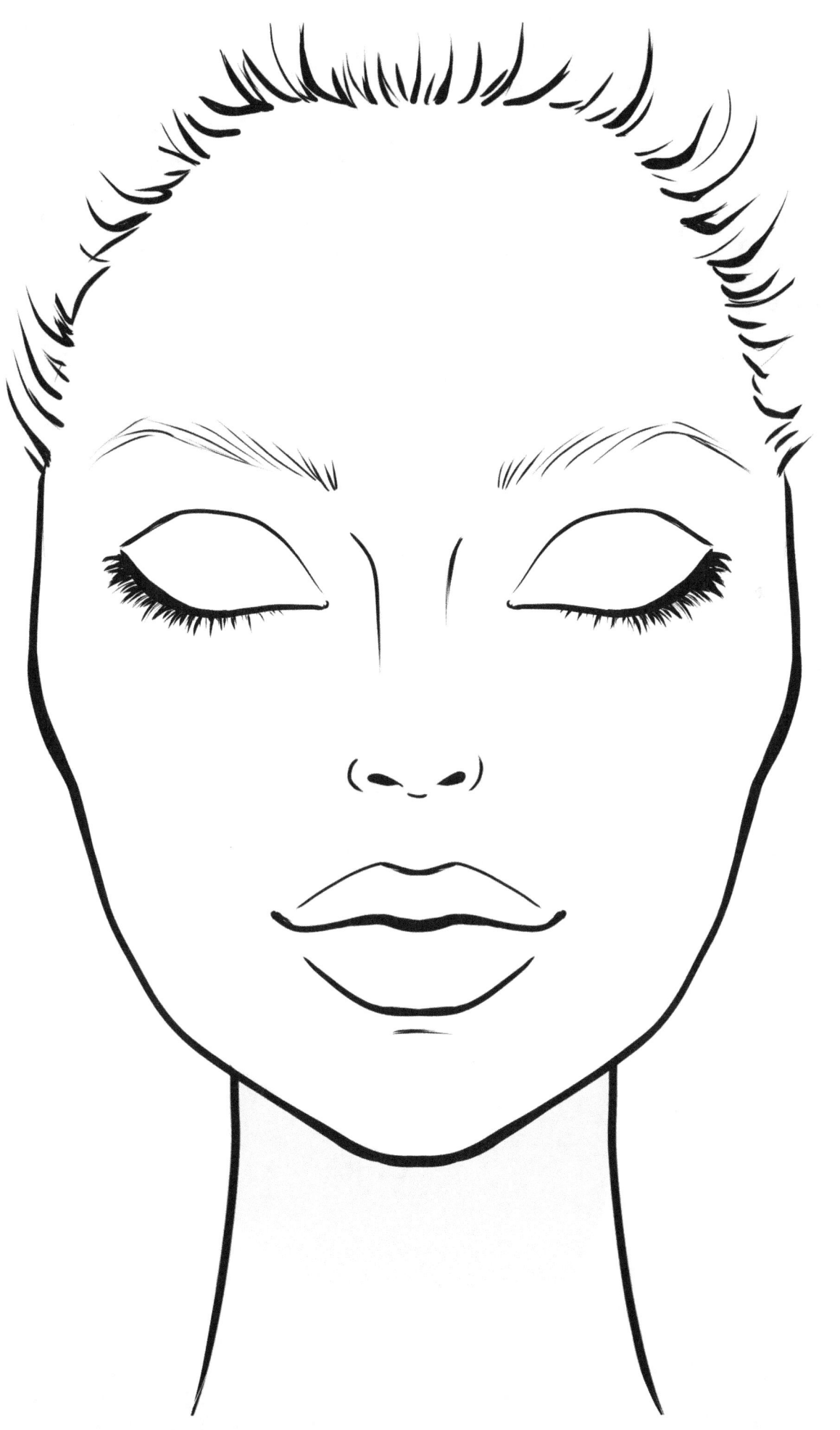

## PREPARATION

Cleanser

---

Moisturizer

---

Primer

---

## FACE

Concealer

---

Foundation

---

Powder

---

Highlighter

---

Contour

---

Bronzer

---

Blush

---

## EYES

Eyeshadow lid

---

Eyeshadow crease

---

Eyeliner

---

Mascara

---

Lashes

---

Brows

---

## LIPS

Lip color

---

Lip liner

---

Lip gloss

---

## OTHER

---

---

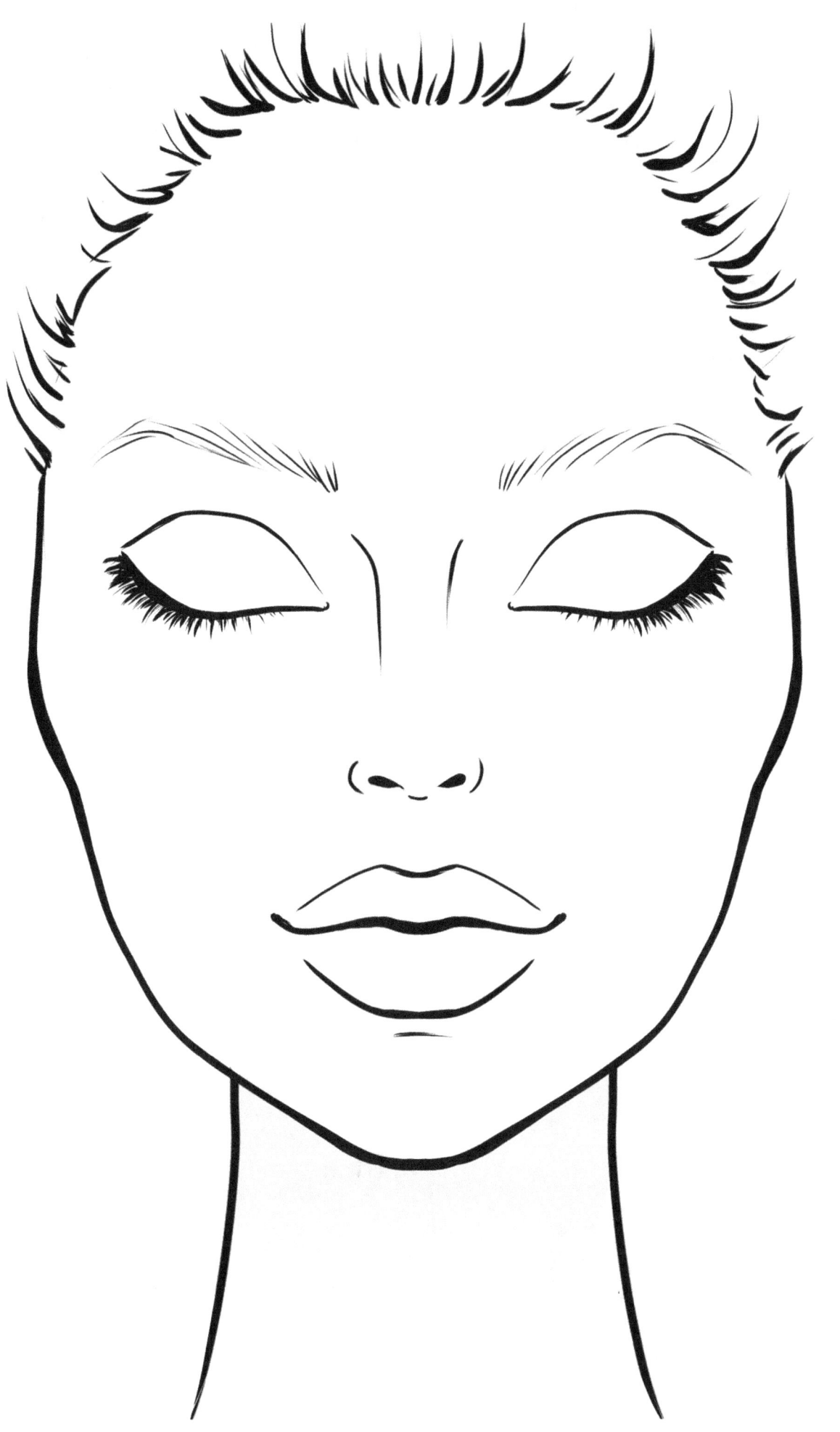

## PREPARATION

Cleanser

---

Moisturizer

---

Primer

---

## FACE

Concealer

---

Foundation

---

Powder

---

Highlighter

---

Contour

---

Bronzer

---

Blush

---

## EYES

Eyeshadow lid

---

Eyeshadow crease

---

Eyeliner

---

Mascara

---

Lashes

---

Brows

---

## LIPS

Lip color

---

Lip liner

---

Lip gloss

---

## OTHER

---

---

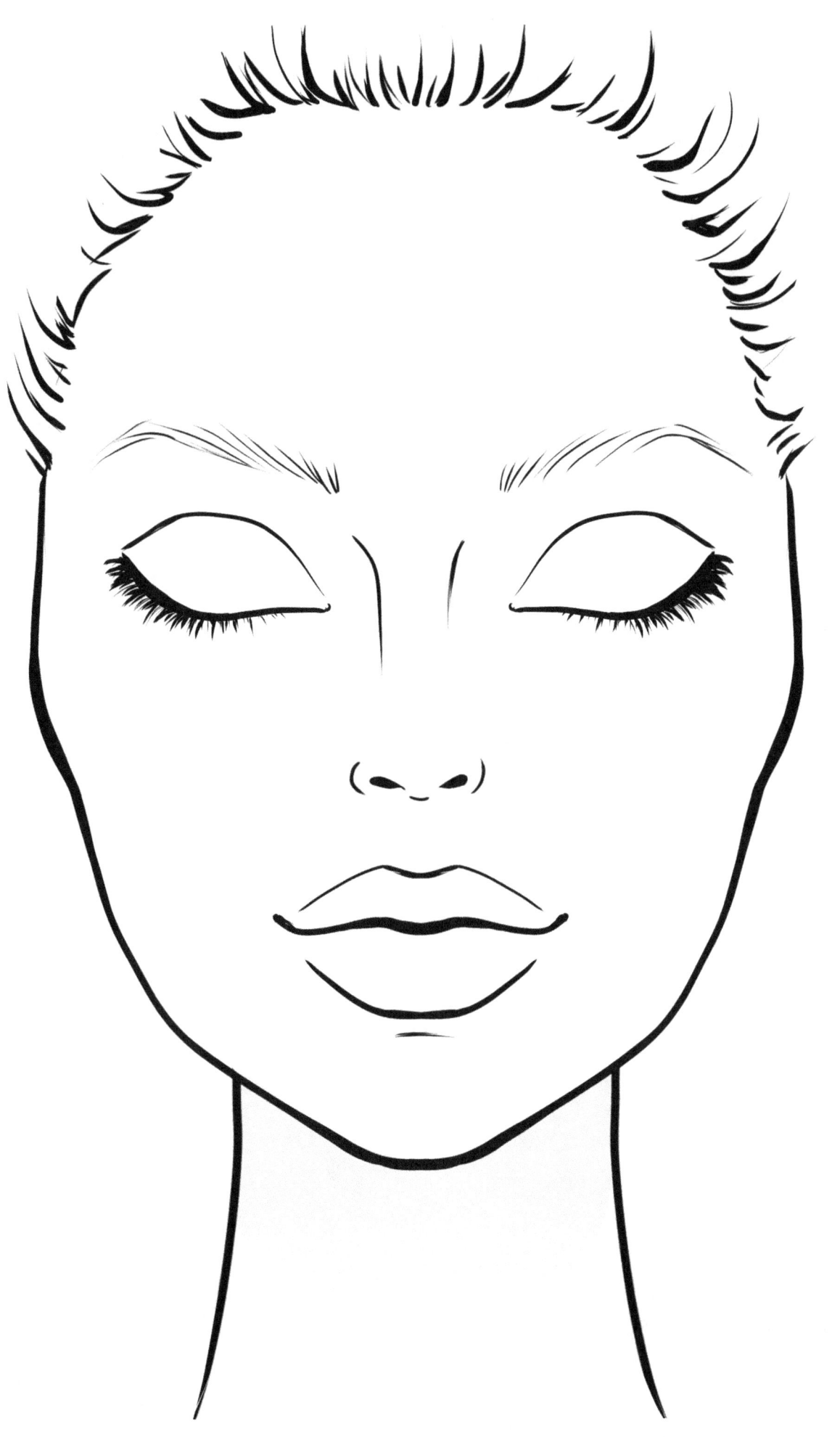

## PREPARATION

Cleanser

---

Moisturizer

---

Primer

---

## FACE

Concealer

---

Foundation

---

Powder

---

Highlighter

---

Contour

---

Bronzer

---

Blush

---

## EYES

Eyeshadow lid

---

Eyeshadow crease

---

Eyeliner

---

Mascara

---

Lashes

---

Brows

---

## LIPS

Lip color

---

Lip liner

---

Lip gloss

---

## OTHER

---

---

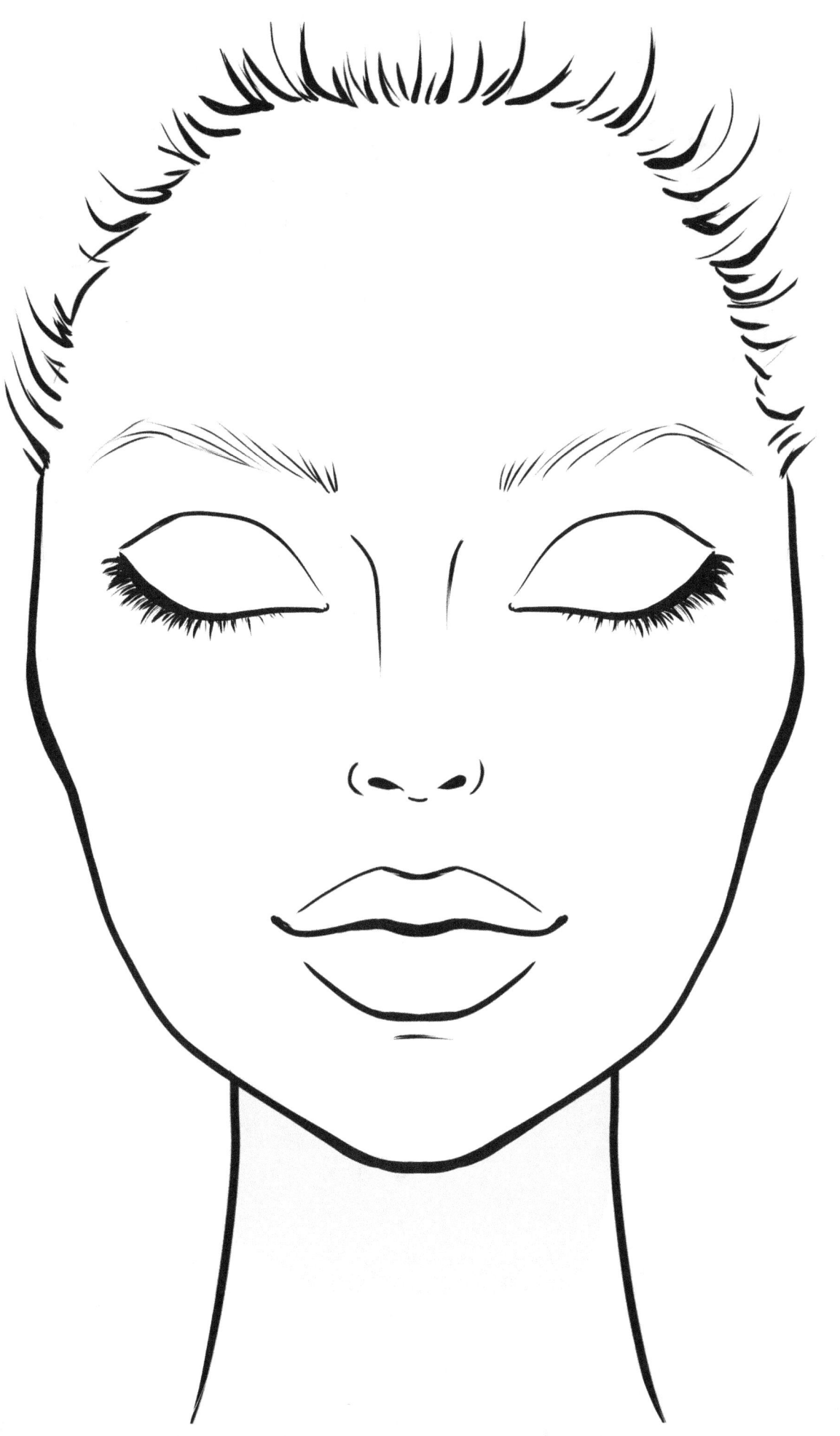

## PREPARATION

Cleanser

------------------------------------

Moisturizer

------------------------------------

Primer

------------------------------------

## FACE

Concealer

------------------------------------

Foundation

------------------------------------

Powder

------------------------------------

Highlighter

------------------------------------

Contour

------------------------------------

Bronzer

------------------------------------

Blush

------------------------------------

## EYES

Eyeshadow lid

------------------------------------

Eyeshadow crease

------------------------------------

Eyeliner

------------------------------------

Mascara

------------------------------------

Lashes

------------------------------------

Brows

------------------------------------

## LIPS

Lip color

------------------------------------

Lip liner

------------------------------------

Lip gloss

------------------------------------

## OTHER

------------------------------------

------------------------------------

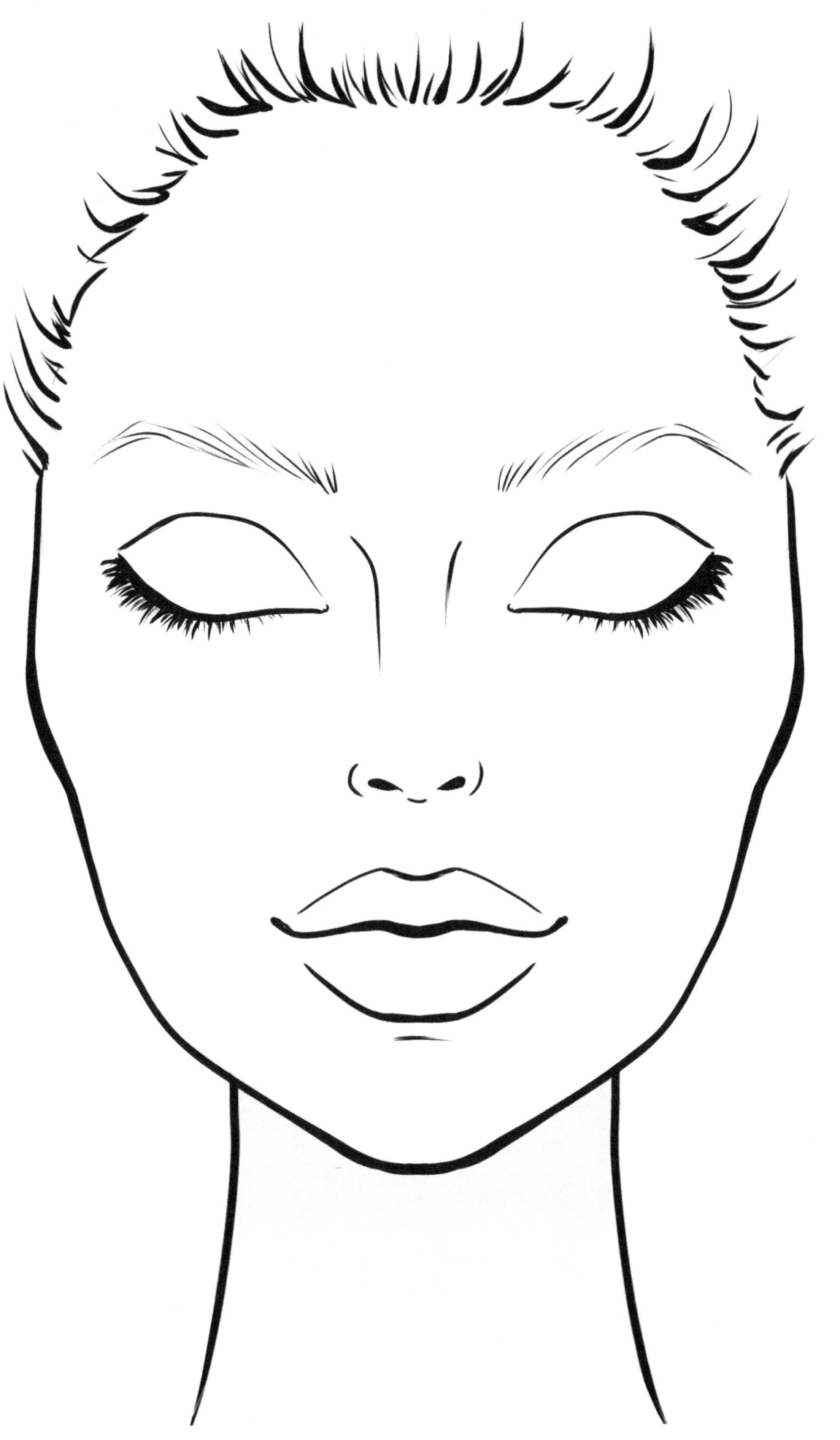

## PREPARATION

Cleanser

----------------------------------------

Moisturizer

----------------------------------------

Primer

----------------------------------------

## FACE

Concealer

----------------------------------------

Foundation

----------------------------------------

Powder

----------------------------------------

Highlighter

----------------------------------------

Contour

----------------------------------------

Bronzer

----------------------------------------

Blush

----------------------------------------

## EYES

Eyeshadow lid

----------------------------------------

Eyeshadow crease

----------------------------------------

Eyeliner

----------------------------------------

Mascara

----------------------------------------

Lashes

----------------------------------------

Brows

----------------------------------------

## LIPS

Lip color

----------------------------------------

Lip liner

----------------------------------------

Lip gloss

----------------------------------------

## OTHER

----------------------------------------

----------------------------------------

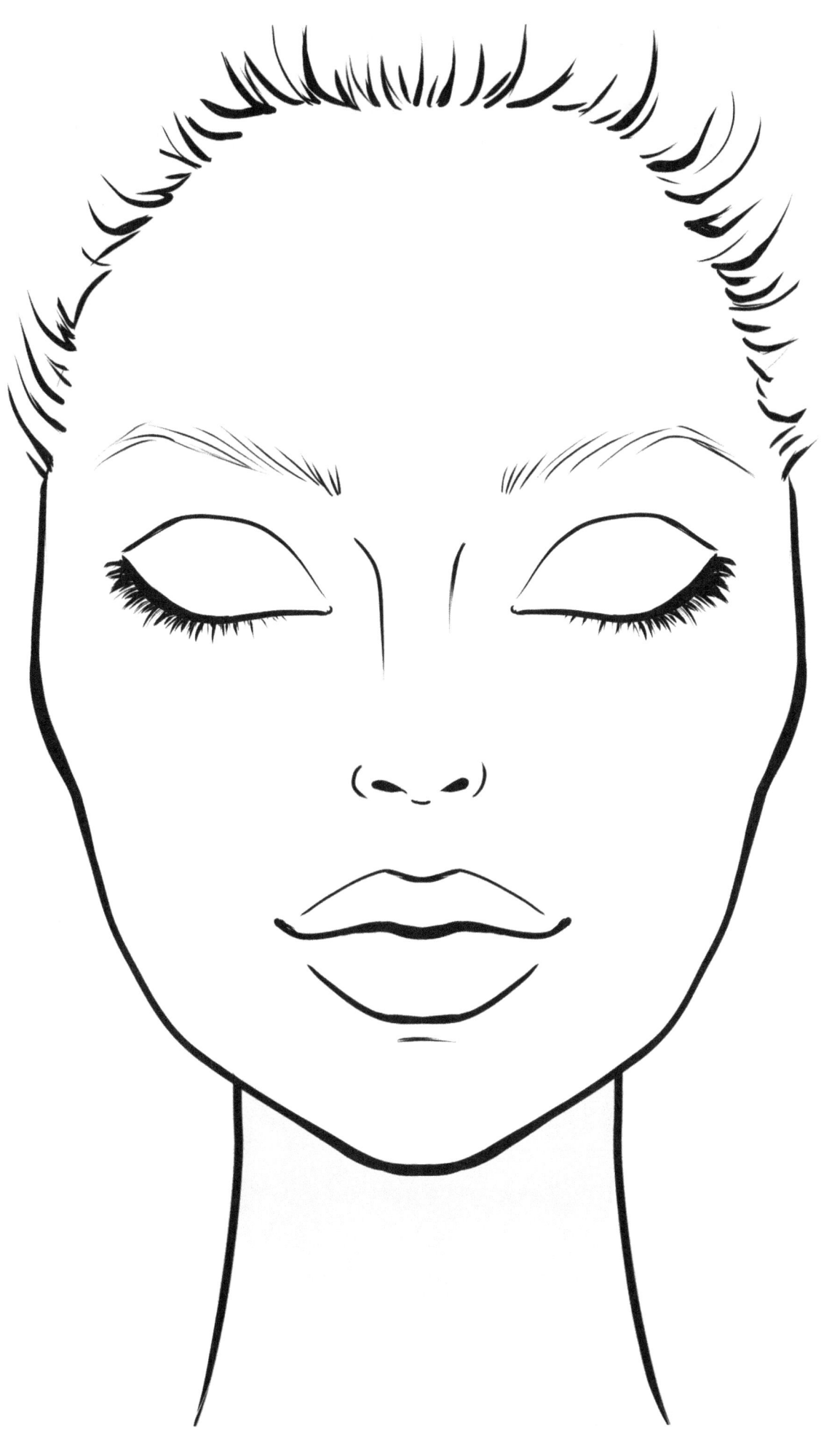

## PREPARATION

Cleanser

-----------------------------------------

Moisturizer

-----------------------------------------

Primer

-----------------------------------------


## FACE

Concealer

-----------------------------------------

Foundation

-----------------------------------------

Powder

-----------------------------------------

Highlighter

-----------------------------------------

Contour

-----------------------------------------

Bronzer

-----------------------------------------

Blush

-----------------------------------------


## EYES

Eyeshadow lid

-----------------------------------------

Eyeshadow crease

-----------------------------------------

Eyeliner

-----------------------------------------

Mascara

-----------------------------------------

Lashes

-----------------------------------------

Brows

-----------------------------------------


## LIPS

Lip color

-----------------------------------------

Lip liner

-----------------------------------------

Lip gloss

-----------------------------------------


## OTHER

-----------------------------------------

-----------------------------------------

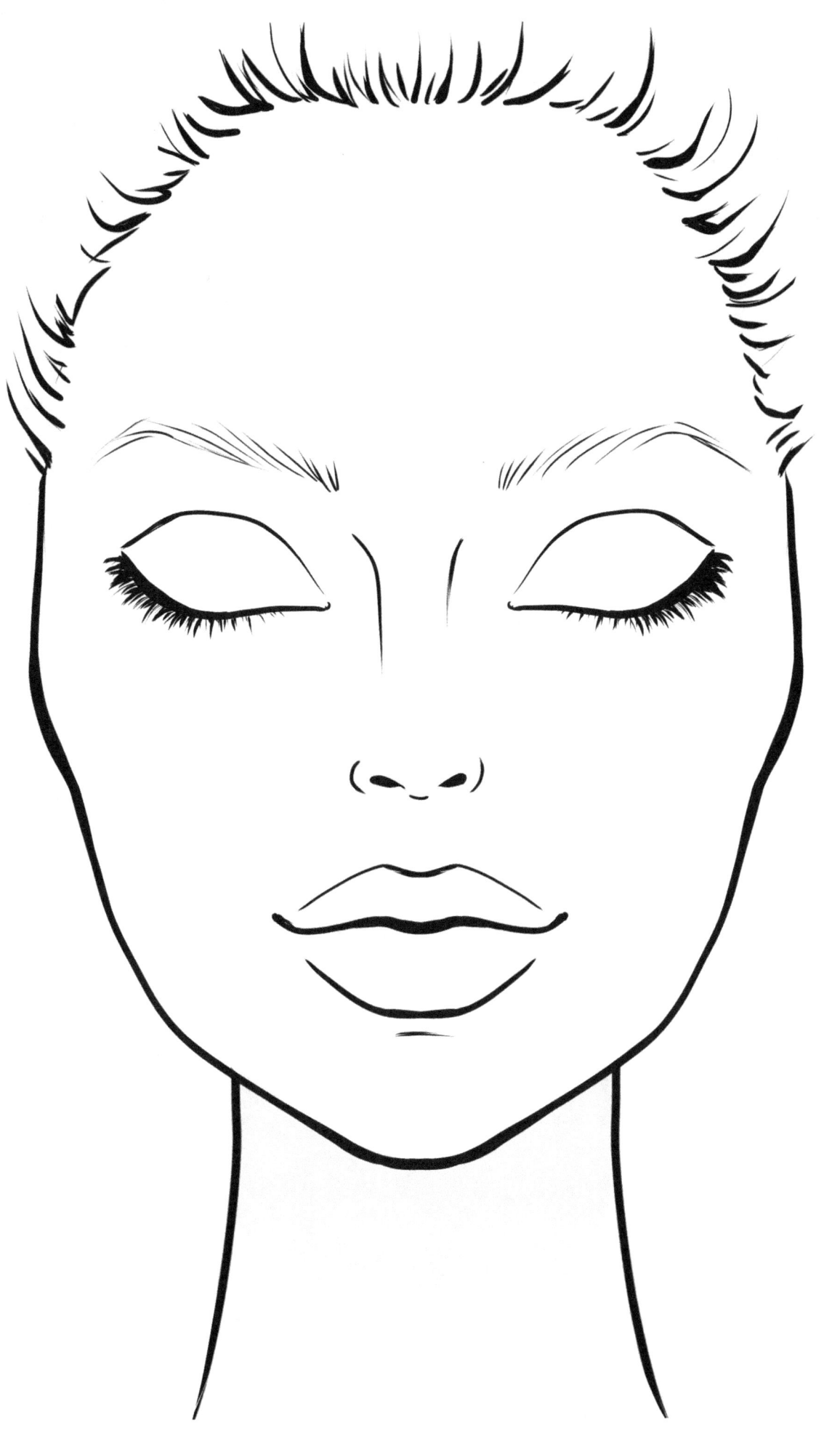

## PREPARATION

Cleanser

---------------------------------

Moisturizer

---------------------------------

Primer

---------------------------------

## FACE

Concealer

---------------------------------

Foundation

---------------------------------

Powder

---------------------------------

Highlighter

---------------------------------

Contour

---------------------------------

Bronzer

---------------------------------

Blush

---------------------------------

## EYES

Eyeshadow lid

---------------------------------

Eyeshadow crease

---------------------------------

Eyeliner

---------------------------------

Mascara

---------------------------------

Lashes

---------------------------------

Brows

---------------------------------

## LIPS

Lip color

---------------------------------

Lip liner

---------------------------------

Lip gloss

---------------------------------

## OTHER

---------------------------------

---------------------------------

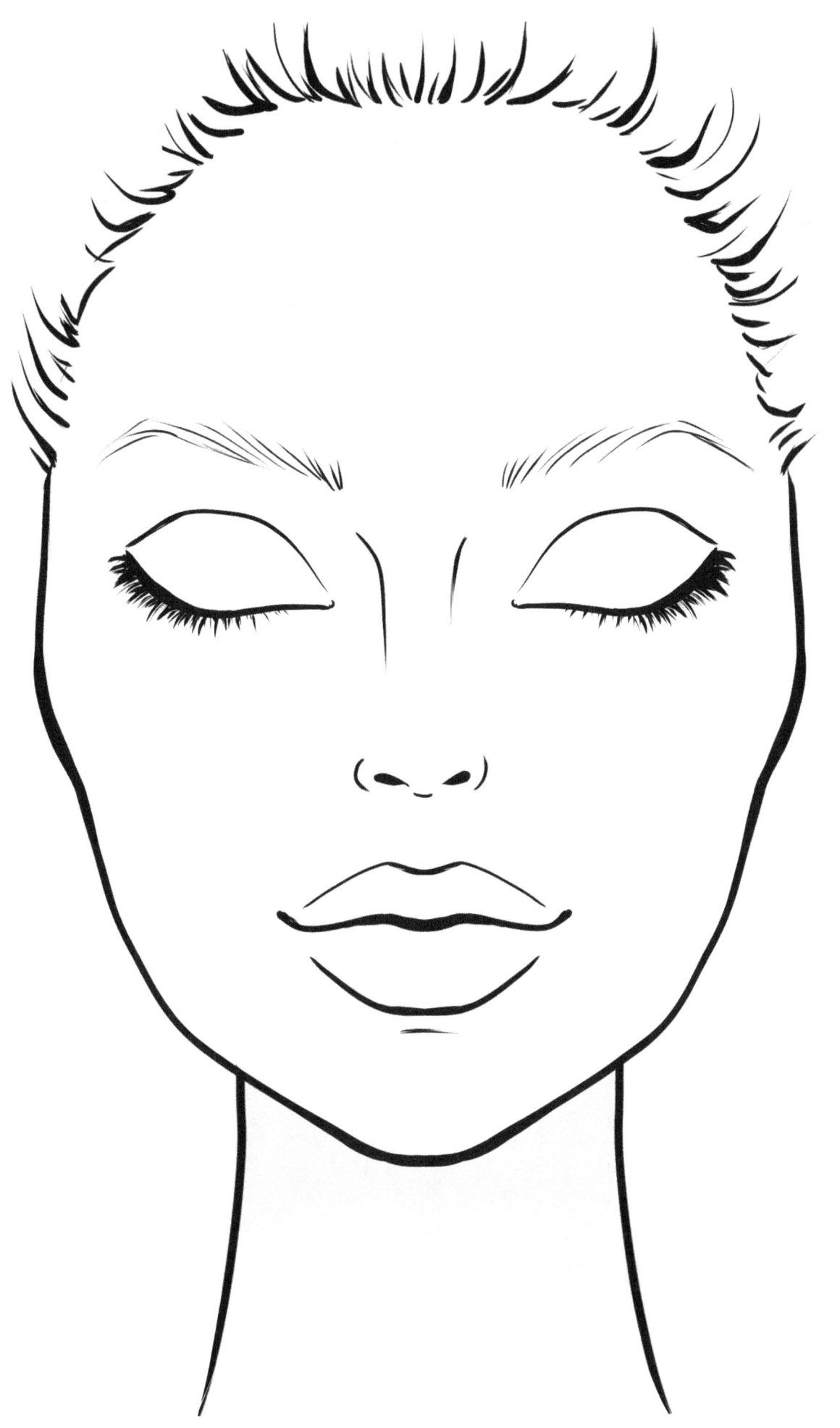

## PREPARATION

Cleanser

-------------------------------------------

Moisturizer

-------------------------------------------

Primer

-------------------------------------------


## FACE

Concealer

-------------------------------------------

Foundation

-------------------------------------------

Powder

-------------------------------------------

Highlighter

-------------------------------------------

Contour

-------------------------------------------

Bronzer

-------------------------------------------

Blush

-------------------------------------------


## EYES

Eyeshadow lid

-------------------------------------------

Eyeshadow crease

-------------------------------------------

Eyeliner

-------------------------------------------

Mascara

-------------------------------------------

Lashes

-------------------------------------------

Brows

-------------------------------------------


## LIPS

Lip color

-------------------------------------------

Lip liner

-------------------------------------------

Lip gloss

-------------------------------------------


## OTHER

-------------------------------------------

-------------------------------------------

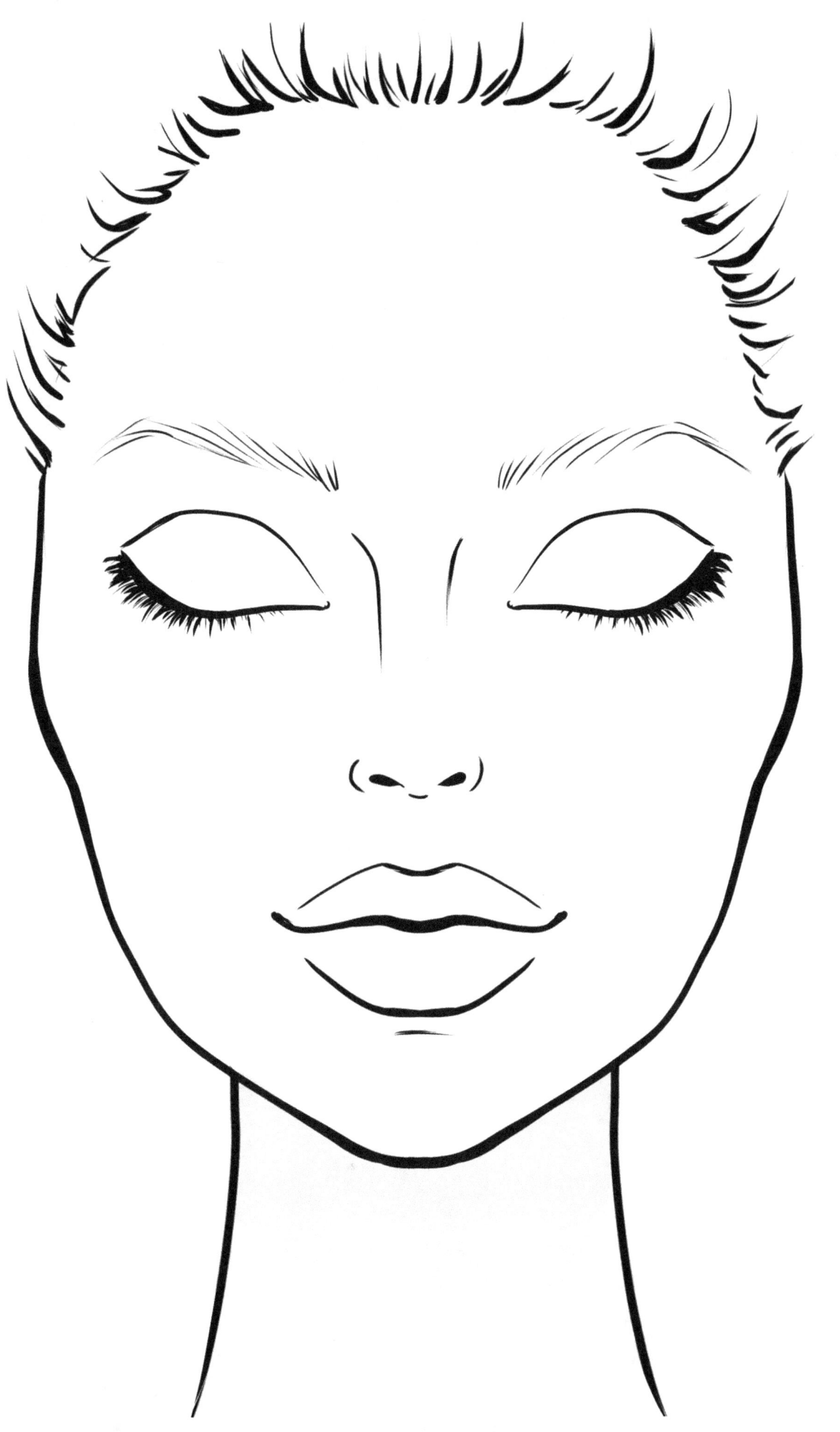

## PREPARATION

Cleanser

------------------------------------

Moisturizer

------------------------------------

Primer

------------------------------------

## FACE

Concealer

------------------------------------

Foundation

------------------------------------

Powder

------------------------------------

Highlighter

------------------------------------

Contour

------------------------------------

Bronzer

------------------------------------

Blush

------------------------------------

## EYES

Eyeshadow lid

------------------------------------

Eyeshadow crease

------------------------------------

Eyeliner

------------------------------------

Mascara

------------------------------------

Lashes

------------------------------------

Brows

------------------------------------

## LIPS

Lip color

------------------------------------

Lip liner

------------------------------------

Lip gloss

------------------------------------

## OTHER

------------------------------------

------------------------------------

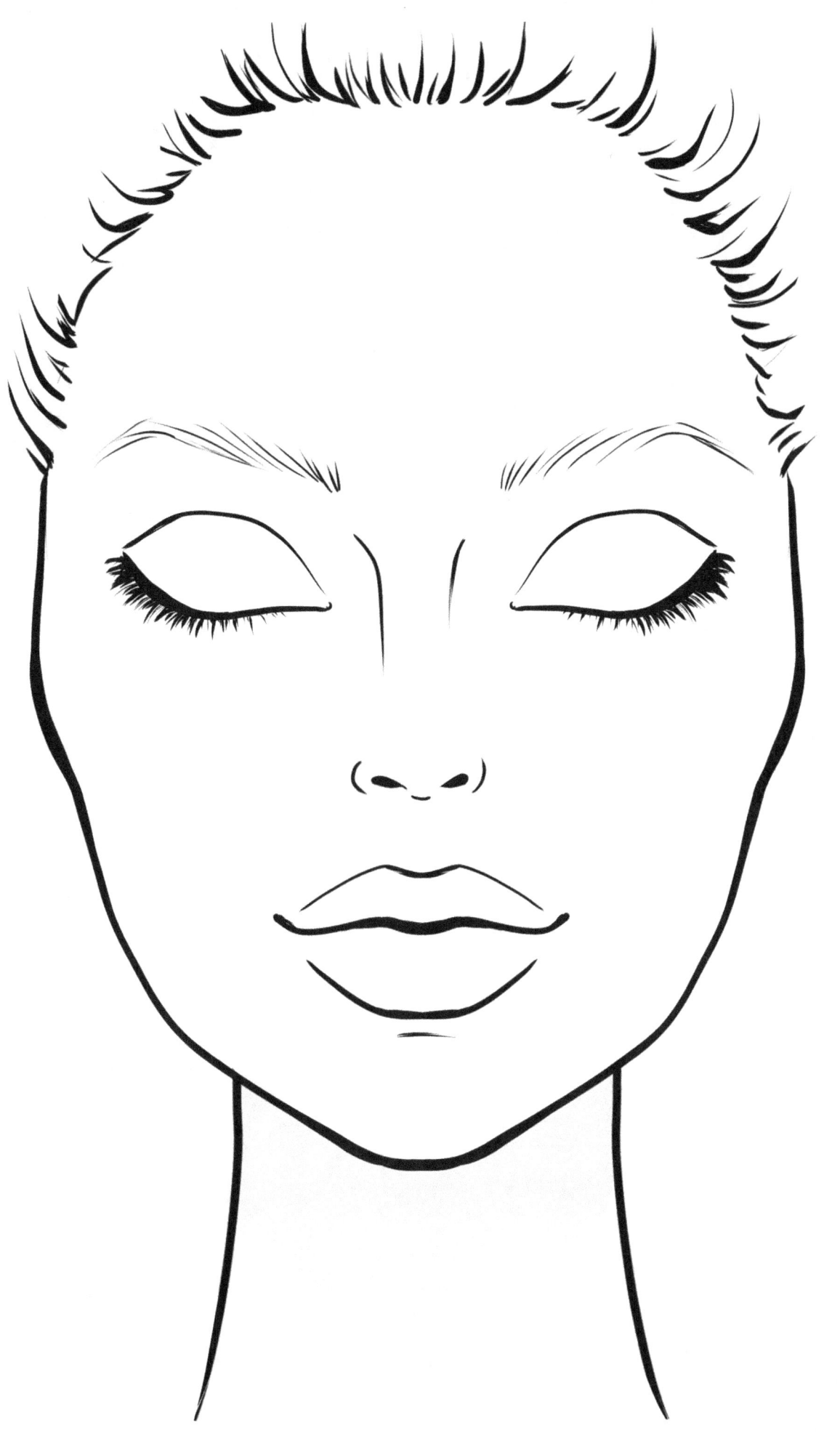

## PREPARATION

Cleanser

---

Moisturizer

---

Primer

---

## FACE

Concealer

---

Foundation

---

Powder

---

Highlighter

---

Contour

---

Bronzer

---

Blush

---

## EYES

Eyeshadow lid

---

Eyeshadow crease

---

Eyeliner

---

Mascara

---

Lashes

---

Brows

---

## LIPS

Lip color

---

Lip liner

---

Lip gloss

---

## OTHER

---

---

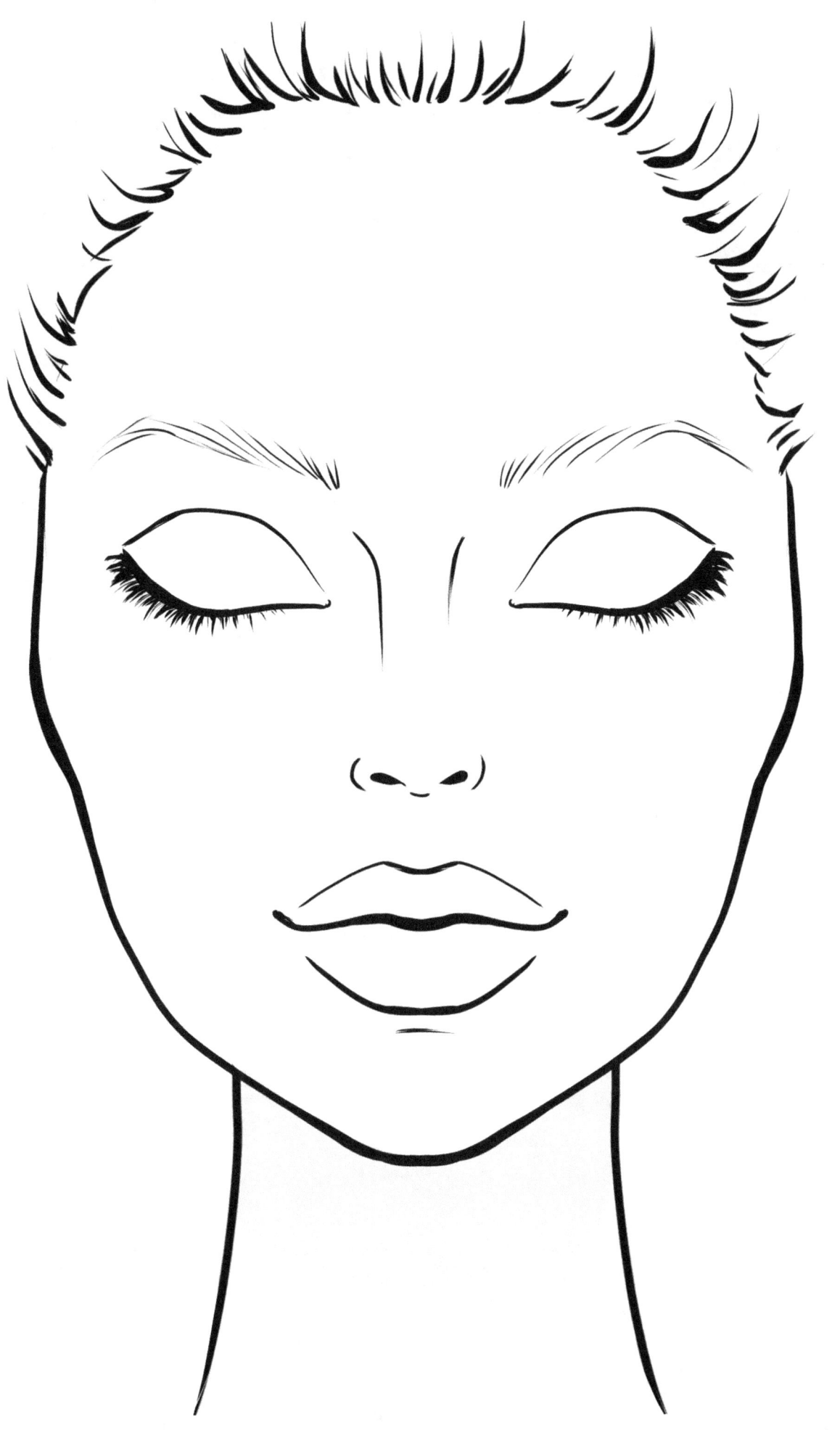

## PREPARATION

Cleanser

-----------------------------------------

Moisturizer

-----------------------------------------

Primer

-----------------------------------------

## FACE

Concealer

-----------------------------------------

Foundation

-----------------------------------------

Powder

-----------------------------------------

Highlighter

-----------------------------------------

Contour

-----------------------------------------

Bronzer

-----------------------------------------

Blush

-----------------------------------------

## EYES

Eyeshadow lid

-----------------------------------------

Eyeshadow crease

-----------------------------------------

Eyeliner

-----------------------------------------

Mascara

-----------------------------------------

Lashes

-----------------------------------------

Brows

-----------------------------------------

## LIPS

Lip color

-----------------------------------------

Lip liner

-----------------------------------------

Lip gloss

-----------------------------------------

## OTHER

-----------------------------------------

-----------------------------------------

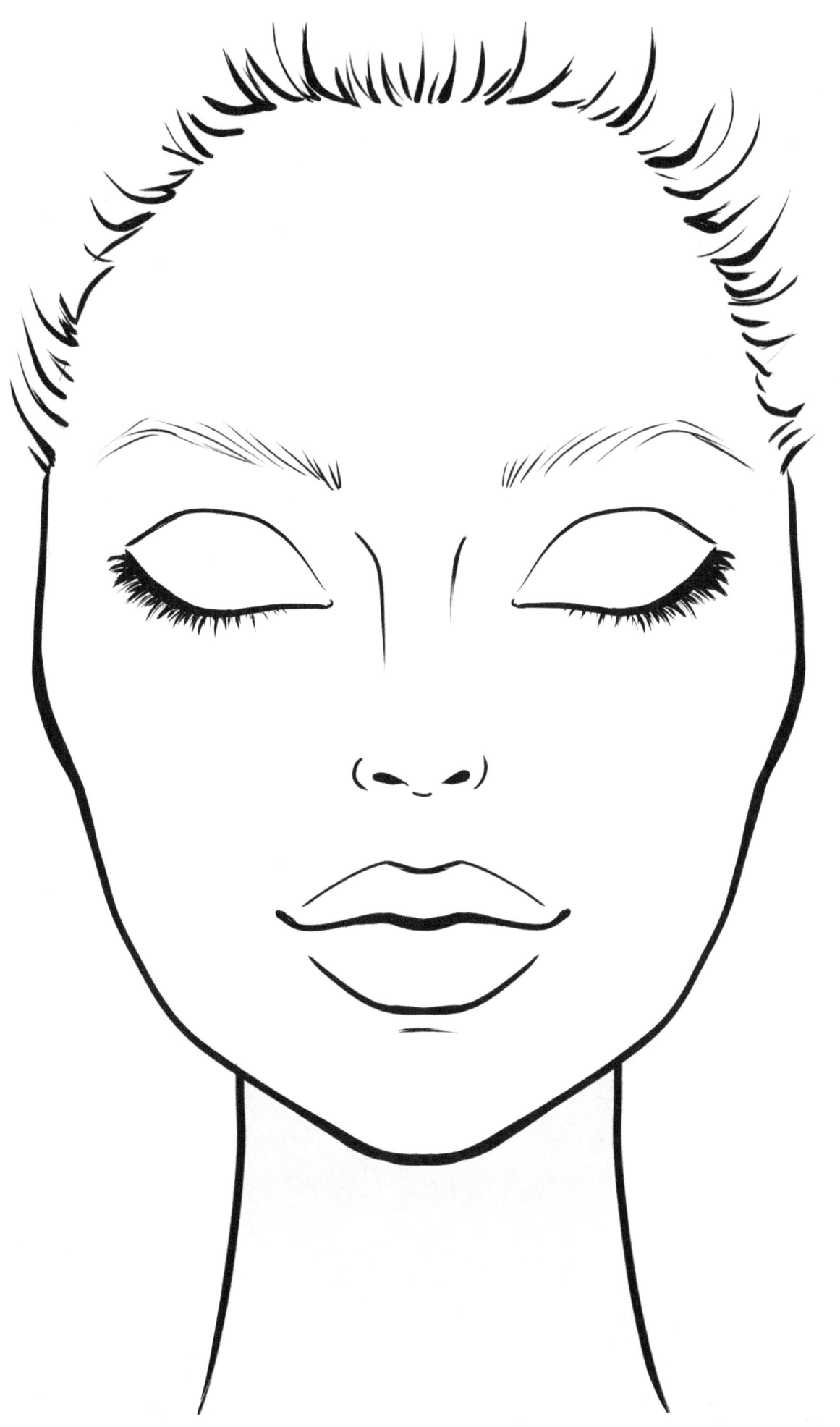

## PREPARATION

Cleanser

---

Moisturizer

---

Primer

---

## FACE

Concealer

---

Foundation

---

Powder

---

Highlighter

---

Contour

---

Bronzer

---

Blush

---

## EYES

Eyeshadow lid

---

Eyeshadow crease

---

Eyeliner

---

Mascara

---

Lashes

---

Brows

---

## LIPS

Lip color

---

Lip liner

---

Lip gloss

---

## OTHER

---

---

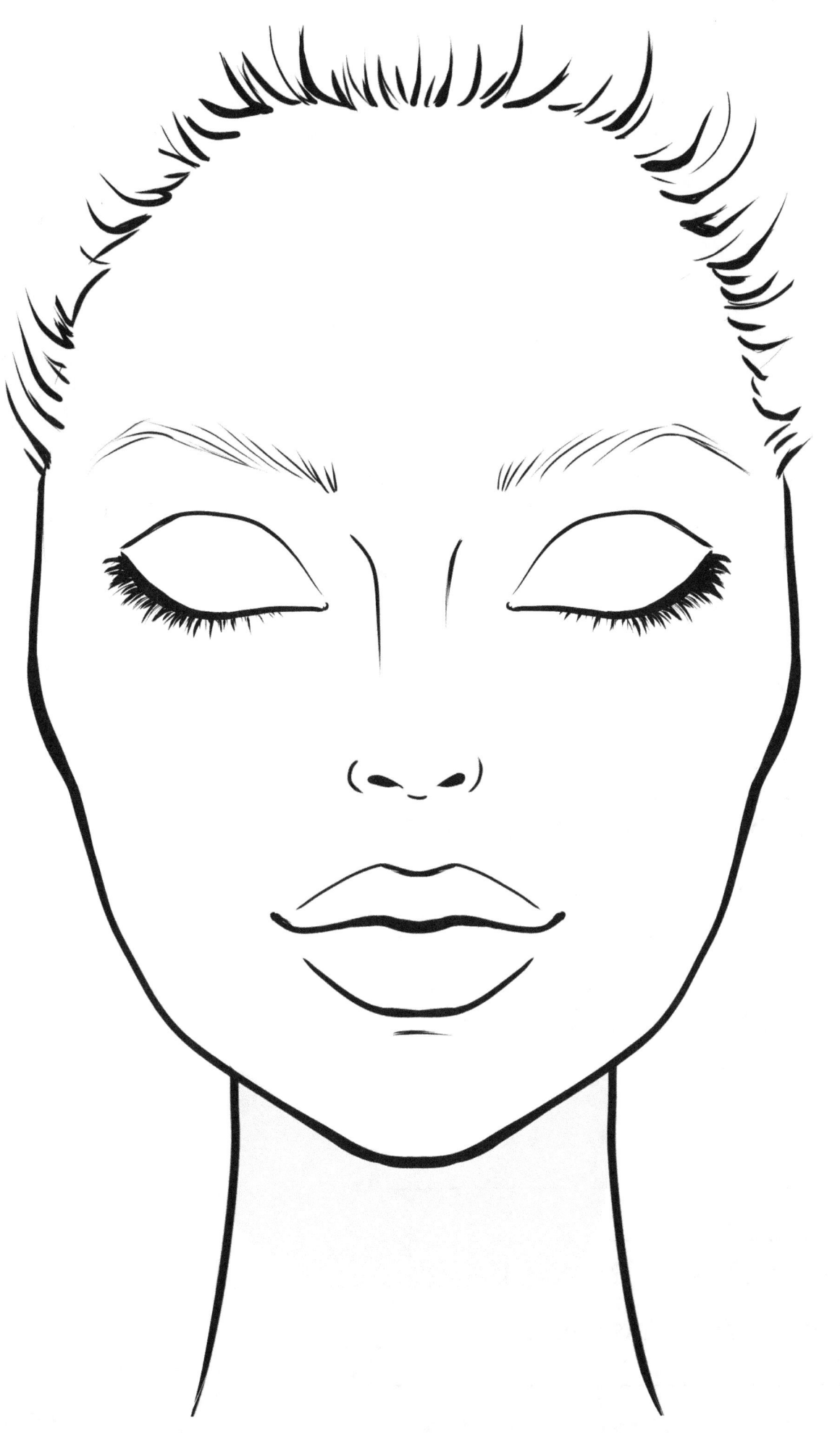

# MORE FROM US:

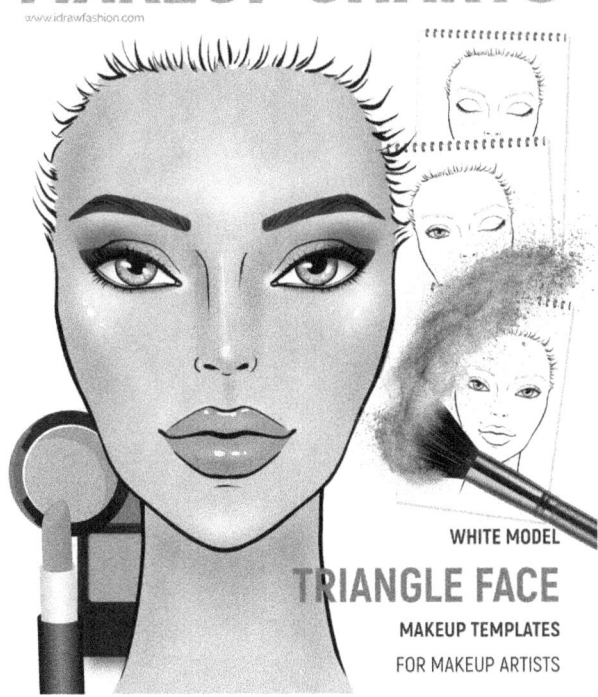

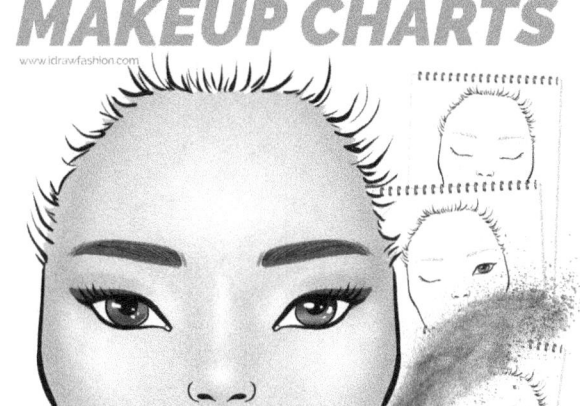

**WHITE MODEL**

## TRIANGLE FACE

MAKEUP TEMPLATES

FOR MAKEUP ARTISTS

**ASIAN MODEL**

## OVAL FACE

MAKEUP TEMPLATES

FOR MAKEUP ARTISTS

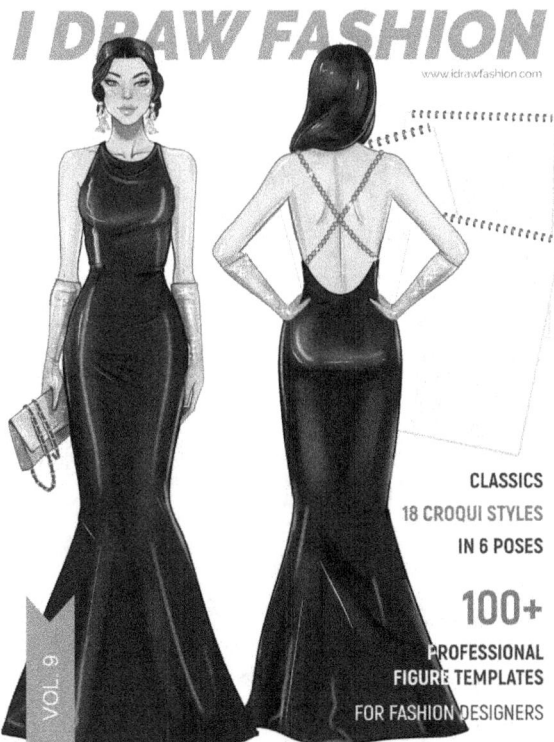

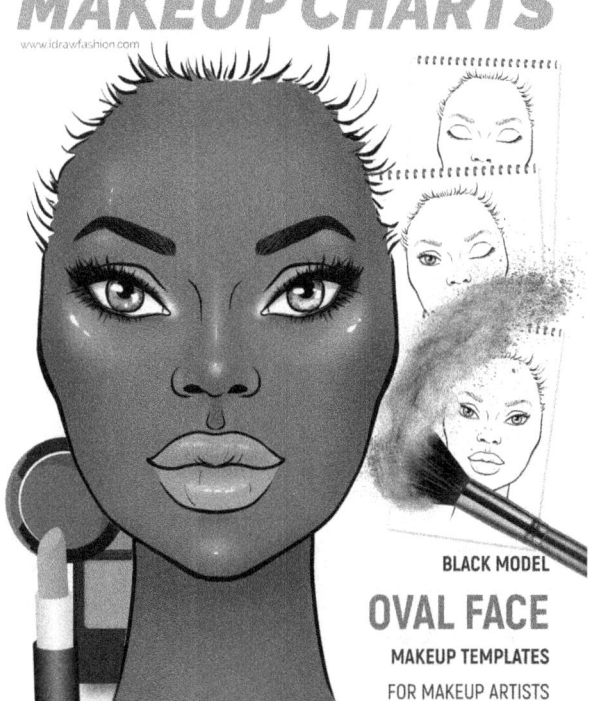

**CLASSICS**

18 CROQUI STYLES

IN 6 POSES

**100+**

PROFESSIONAL

FIGURE TEMPLATES

FOR FASHION DESIGNERS

**BLACK MODEL**

## OVAL FACE

MAKEUP TEMPLATES

FOR MAKEUP ARTISTS